The TRAPS THAT SATAN LAID

Overcoming the Devil and Other Demons with the Power of Jesus Christ

Danica Ked

BALBOA. PRESS
A DIVISION OF HAY HOUSE

Balboa Press books may be ordered through booksellers or by contacting:

Balboa Press
A Division of Hay House
1663 Liberty Drive
Bloomington, IN 47403
www.balboapress.com.au
1 (877) 407-4847

Scripture taken from the King James Version of the Bible

Print information available on the last page.

ISBN: 978-1-5043-1018-5 (sc)
ISBN: 978-1-5043-1019-2 (e)

Balboa Press rev. date: 09/12/2017

ACKNOWLEDGEMENTS

I'm a servant of Jesus Christ, and I want to thank the Lord and acknowledge him for delivering me out of Satan's kingdom and bringing me back into his marvellous light. I wrote this book to expose the unfruitful deeds of darkness and to inform you through my own personal experiences of what Satan can do to a true born-again Christian. Without the Lord's intervention, I most likely wouldn't have been able to write this testimony. I pray that this book opens your eyes to the truth.

I want to thank Joshua, my husband, for staying by my side after everything I did against him. He assisted me in editing this book and supported me as I wrote it. Thank you for your love and support.

To my two beautiful girls, Violet and Ruby, I just want to say thank you for helping Mummy through this horrible time. Without the two of you, I would have given up on life. You both kept me going through it all. This has shown me what a mother will go through for the love of her children.

To the rest of my family and friends, thank you for all your love and support.

CHAPTER 1

GROWING UP

GROWING UP WAS a fun time for me. I grew up on a dead-end street, with our house being directly opposite the park grounds, which had open fields and bike tracks. In our street and surrounding streets lived kids our own age. We introduced ourselves and became friends. All of us grew up together, and we would often go over each other's houses and play games like soccer, volleyball, cricket, and tennis. We would fly kites in the open park and hang around each other and talk. At this stage, life was a breeze, and I didn't have a worry in the world.

During my childhood, my sister, Sally (real names are not used in this book), and I decided to visit a friend who lived a few doors down from us. Some of the neighbourhood kids were over too. As we were inside their garage, they secretly brought out a Ouija board, also known as a spirit board. Sally and I didn't participate in this game. However, we hung around and watched. Our friends sat down in a circle around the board and brought out a glass cup. They all breathed into the glass cup and placed it on the board. I saw how the glass lifted off the board while each person placed a finger on it. A spirit had entered the glass, causing it to hover over the board game. When they asked the spirit questions, the glass would hover over "yes" or "no" or move to each letter and spell out a word. At this stage, I didn't know what this game was. This game is from the occult, and being a Christian from birth, I had decided not to join in. This was the first spirit I ever encountered.

One morning, when I was seven, my father was heading off to work when he saw me standing still and foaming at the mouth. I could not comprehend anything. He immediately called an ambulance, which rushed me to hospital. They said I had had a seizure. My grandmother, May, sat by my bedside at the hospital and told me that I had been walking around the hospital, unaware of my surroundings or who I was. After I came to my senses, I ended up spending one week in hospital. I remember waking up and coming out of the darkness. Suddenly, I became aware of my surroundings, and my comprehension returned.

The doctors put me on medication. However, it hindered my ability to study. As a result, my year 2 teacher decided that I should be held back. My mother intervened in the school's decision and asked them to see how I would do in the following year. They accepted her request and allowed me to enter the next grade. Once I was taken off the medication, I was able to study well again. You see, if I had repeated the year, I wouldn't have met Joshua, my husband, and had our two children with him. My high school friend introduced me to him, and we ended up getting married.

When I was a young child, my parents, Emily and Luke, decided to put a cartoon on the television for us to watch. They thought it was innocent and did not see the underlying storyline of the film, which was filled with sorcery and evil. The cartoon was about a young boy who was possessed by an evil spirit. This young boy was evil, and the good guys stopped him by casting the demon out of him. As a result, he became good. I remember how annoyed I became at the end of this cartoon. I hated it and wanted the evil character back. Something about this boy made me like evil. He had power, and his mannerism was controlling. As a result, I was drawn towards him.

Our family grew up in a Christian household. We were of the

Pentecostal faith until my father converted to the Message Believers. This church held the teaching of William Branham. These people claimed he was a prophet, and my father started following their doctrines. We attended a church every Sunday; my uncle Tim was the pastor. It was the smallest church I had ever seen. It only had a handful of members, and we were basically the only children attending. We were bored at church as children. Deep down, I wanted to attend my grandmother's church. It had children my own age, and I found it more interesting. It was one of the true churches, and God was present there. When I did attend my grandmother's church, a person would stand up and give prophecies. This person would speak out the prophecy as she received it, which edified the church. This fascinated me. However, one day, my grandmother's church closed down and the congregation separated into other churches. Some of the members of this church started to attend a Slavic Assemblies of God church, which was where my grandmother also decided to attend.

I rarely prayed as a child, but one night I prayed, "Lord, could you give me wisdom like Solomon?" I don't know why I asked the Lord for wisdom. However, as I was growing up, the Lord opened my eyes to a lot of things. I even tried hard to avoid entering the world, until Satan drew me away from God.

In the early 1990s, my mother was diagnosed with motor neurone disease. She was in her early thirties when she became sick. My parents began seeking deliverance through prayer meetings and healing services; one day, a Christian brother prayed over her and received a vision. He told her that he saw an open grave and saw her being in the resurrection. She wanted to live out her life and did not want to pass away at such a young age. She hoped that God would heal her from the disease, but in 1993, my mother passed away at the age of thirty-two.

Grandmother May, was a big help to my parents. While my mother was sick, she often came over and took care of my father and three siblings. One morning, I woke up early and walked into my parents' bedroom; I lay down next to my mother as my father went to work. Shortly after, I woke up and walked out of the room, without looking at her. I didn't speak to her or say anything and just left the room; the only thing I can recall is looking at the clock, which read 6:00 a.m. This was the day she died.

I believe the Lord pulled me out of the room that day. I would've been extremely afraid to witness my mother's death. I got ready for school earlier than I normally would have. Usually, I would wait for my grandmother to wake me up, but that day was different. When my grandmother went to check on my mother, she yelled out in pain, and it shocked me. I remember running into my bedroom, covering my head, and crying out to God, "Please, Lord, no, no!" I knew my mother had passed away.

It was a horrible time for all of us, and it took me a long time to get over her death. For some unknown reason, I started to completely lose my memory. I can hardly recall anything of my mother now, and this worries me. My memory loss is like amnesia. I can recall some events, but a large part of my memory seems to have been completely erased. I just can't recall them at all.

As a child, I loved the Lord with all my heart, and I used to sing to the Lord. One of the songs I would sing was "In the Name of Jesus." I never listened to secular music, and my father taught me that evolution goes against God. He would give me creation magazines to read and showed us documentaries on creation versus evolution. The Bible teaches that the Lord created everything in six days and rested on the seventh day.

We once rented a movie with evil content throughout it. It was a very dark film for kids at the time, and I remember how the scenes shocked me. These types of films led me down a darker road in my life, and I started to watch horror films and supernatural television series. When I was a teenager, I used to record some of these shows behind my father's back. I really wanted to watch these shows, but I didn't want to risk my father stopping me. This was how I slipped away from God. And before I realised it, Satan had a hold on me.

Sometimes after church, we would go to my cousin's place. He owned a collection of popular children's novels. The storylines of these novels were all supernaturally themed. I would take one each time I visited him and read them. At that young age, it never occurred to me to stay away from such things, and no one stopped me from reading them, nor did they confiscate them.

My grandmother is a Christian who has left the world to serve the Lord. May doesn't watch television or celebrate any holidays, and she prays and fasts often. She also prays in tongues and is truly out of the world. She has had some influence over my life. However, we differ in doctrines. She holds the doctrines of "Jesus only" or "Oneness," and she always told me not to watch television. But as a young child, I ignored her complaining. One day, she told me a story of how her sister, my great-aunt Julie, was attacked by demons in her apartment. Aunt Julie wasn't a Christian at this stage, but after so many demonic attacks, she came to Christ. This story of how she was terrorised by demons stuck with me all my life. She saw a demonic-looking dwarf in her apartment and was tormented by demons. During these attacks, she asked a Christian brother to pray over her, as well as covering the house with oil. She was then set free from further attacks. God delivered her.

One day, we visited Great-Aunt Julie's place, and while on my visit, I looked up and saw this hole in the wall which was previously used as an electrical power point; live wiring was exposed. As I stared at it, I fell into a trance and felt the presence of a spirit, luring me towards this exposed hole to electrocute myself. Someone interrupted me and woke me out of this trance. This was the first time a spirit tried to kill me. I truly believe God helped me at that moment.

My cousin Samantha was haunted by a demon.

"I see a man following me when I go to sleep," she said, in a fearful tone.

It frightened her a lot. My mother's family had a history of the supernatural, both from the Lord and from the devil. I went to visit another cousin of mine named Felicity, and she revealed to me that her brother Tom had been haunted by a being at a young age.

"Tom sees a man at the edge of his bed at night," Felicity told me. "He stands at the bed with his arms together," she continued describing the man. "Tom is not able to see his face, just the back of his body."

I was horrified and quickly said, "It has to be a demon."

"No, Tom thinks it's just his mental health," she replied.

My grandfather Darren passed away a good number of years ago. He walked with the Lord as a Christian and received prophecies. Before the war broke out in his homeland, my grandfather was told by the Lord to leave the country. He obeyed God and left Yugoslavia with his family. One day during prayer, my grandfather received word from the Lord. "As many children as your daughter has, I will save them all," he said to my grandfather. Knowing about this prophecy growing up, it seemed like a normal thing to me, and I didn't appreciate the meaning behind it until now. This daughter was my mother, and the prophecy was about my siblings and me. The Lord told my grandfather that he was going to save us all. My brothers, however, slipped away from the Lord, but if this truly was from God, it will come to pass.

My great-grandfather John was the first member of our family who came to Christ. Before this, he was a Muslim, but he decided to convert to Christianity after a Christian man witnessed to him about Jesus. I couldn't imagine not growing up as a Christian, and I thank the Lord for this. God also healed a sick person through my great-grandfather.

My parents could not decide what to name my youngest brother. He did not have a name for about a month after he was born. God spoke to my mother in a dream and said, "Give this child the name Samuel." My parents both agreed and named him Samuel.

Grandmother May was raised a Christian but left God during her marriage. One day, she had a severe stomach pain that brought her to the point of death. She said, "Lord, if you heal me now, I will serve you all my life."

She felt the power of God heal her and instantly came back to the Lord that day; she has been serving the Lord ever since. She was given the gift of tongues later in her life.

I remember something weird took place when I was a child, and it had to do with the front door. I wondered what was behind the door. A UFO came to mind. *Was I remembering this right?* I thought to myself. I recently asked my grandmother about this strange event, which took place one evening at our house, and she confirmed it to me.

She said, "One evening, Emily, Julie, and myself were out in the backyard at your place when we witnessed a UFO fly one metre above the house." My grandmother attracted my attention with this and continued, "I saw a round circular disc with colourful lights flashing around it, and in the window were these green-looking creatures."

My own memory of this was only the front door and our family racing to the front of the house, looking into the open park for an unidentified flying object.

One day, Grandmother May asked me, "Who is God?"

I quickly pondered my brain, and a song named "His Name Is Wonderful" came to mind. I answered, "Jesus!"

It's because of the lyrics to this song, which stated he was "Mighty God"; unfortunately, I denied the Father, not understanding. Grandmother May never corrected me, because this was the answer she wanted to hear from me. As I started to read the Bible, I realised that Jesus is the Word of God who was manifested in the flesh. The Word was with God in the beginning, and the Word is God. Jesus is the Son of God, everlasting Father, and Almighty God because the Father and Jesus are one, but they are also separate, like a son is separate from his father. The Bible states that Jesus sits on the right hand of the Father, who is God.

"In the beginning was the Word, and the Word was with

God, and the Word was God. The same was in the beginning with God. All things were made by him; and without him was not anything made that was made." (John 1:1–3)

My grandmother was determined to make sure I knew that there was only one God, which is true, but as I came to Christ, I could see just how complicated the Lord was.

"For there are three who bear record in heaven, The Father, the Word and the Holy Spirit: and these three are one." (1 John 5:7)

CHAPTER 2

MALADAPTIVE DAYDREAMING DISORDER

IT ALL STARTED to go extremely wrong at the age of eleven. I sat at church, not listening to the sermon, and suddenly had the ability to enter deep inside a dream world (which also is the spirit world).

I used to become extremely bored when it came to preaching, and I would pick up the Bible in church and read some of it to pass the time. I just couldn't pay attention to the preaching; my attention span was bad. I would try to focus, but I always ended up drifting away in my thoughts. I would also sneak out to the bathroom. One time, I looked into the mirror and said, "I don't want to go to church when I'm older." Church really annoyed me, and it felt like a waste of time. As I sat in church one Sunday afternoon, I saw this invisible thing come upon me, and from that moment on, I was able to daydream while awake in a very detailed and deep way. This fantasy world just came to me, and it would take me away from the word of God. This world started off as a childhood fantasy, but down the years, it became extremely dark and evil.

When I was a child, I was given a doll as a gift, and I kept it inside the box for a few years. Sometime after I started daydreaming,

I decided to open the box and play with this doll in a sexual way; this opened the door to sin. This particular doll just suddenly appeared inside my fantasy world. After she entered my life, my storyline changed drastically. It was no longer a childhood fantasy that I was entering into. I quickly attached myself to her and used her to become the main character. I named her Blade Destiny Star, and she would take me into a very dark tunnel, deep into this dark world of demonic daydreaming.

This daydream world was semi-realistic. It was like watching a computer-animated film, in which you could interact with all the characters, just like using an avatar in a video game. I would use the characters which Satan gave me to interact with my character, and although I didn't create her, I used this main character to act out the scenes of the story. I had a lot of demonic influence with all the scenes and characters. I used to open my eyes and see into this world, and it would start up and just take off right in front of my eyes, almost like a vision. I would then enter this world and go deep inside it, separating out reality from this fantasy world.

At this stage, I didn't realise that it was influenced by Satan. It was a world that I thought I created all by myself until recently, when God opened my eyes to what I was doing. I was using my imagination to help me move this dream world in the direction I wanted my story to head towards. However, I was daydreaming in a demonic world that I thought was just part of my mind, and me controlling this world that I thought I created.

One day, I asked myself this question: "How can you subconsciously design a world, using your mind with the help of your imagination, without thinking or making up any of these images?"

The images just come to me. People believe it's just your mind alone performing this task, but after daydreaming for twenty-two years, I can tell you that I never once came up with any of the actual daydreaming designs: the people I interacted with or the background or the colours. When I used my imagination, I would enter into the dream world. I did control a part with my mind. I would initiate the storyline, and then the images would come to me. I also controlled where I wanted to go, what I wanted to do, or who I wanted to see, and the scene would just appear in front of my eyes, allowing me to act out the desires of my heart in a detailed way or creating a detailed storyline that would always end up with evil or exciting twists within this state. When you dream, are you in your subconscious? This is what I used to think until recently. However, my experience in the dream world opened my eyes to the truth. Satan will, at some point, take over your dreams and imagination for his own schemes and purposes.

The Bible tells us to cast down our imaginations, and it's clear that God doesn't like us using it:

"Casting down imaginations, and every high thing that exalteth itself against the knowledge of God, and bringing into captivity every thought to the obedience of Christ." (2 Corinthians 10:5)

My world was science fiction, mixed with drama, horror, supernatural themes, and action. It is hard to describe exactly, but imagine having a semi realistic computer-animated movie where you could talk to the characters in an interactive way and develop deep emotions towards each of them. It was a way of resting my mind through entertainment and also taking my mind off my own reality. I knew the difference and in no way confused the two. I understood that this was a fantasy world, and I entered into it almost every day.

I will describe my world which consumed my life for twenty-two years. I can't describe every detail, but I will explain my world to you and try my best to show you this is truly a demonic condition. The world knows this as maladaptive daydreaming disorder or excessive daydreaming, but the truth is Satan had a lot to do with this fantasy world; the way I received it, I felt it enter into me. I know now that I was interacting with evil, and they would take over some of my scenes and put such heavy satanic influence in them. It would be saturated with evil. This storyline began when I stopped playing with dolls; I opened my eyes and went into this world of fantasy.

Blade was the main character I controlled. She was pretty with a perfect body and was extremely fit. She had red hair and blue eyes and looked like my doll. She wore black clothes consisting of a black top that didn't cover her belly button and black leather pants and boots. Her transportation of choice consisted of a black motorcycle, which could convert into another vehicle. She was secretly a superhero. She was a half-human and half-alien being with a powerful human body that withstood any weapon on Earth.

Her biological father was a king from a light world who came to Earth. He looked human but had incredible power. He had a one-night affair with a human girl, and she became pregnant. He left Earth and returned back to his world without understanding that she was pregnant with his unborn child. Blade was the king's first child. The king had a ring of power which would automatically pass on to the true heir, and no one could take the throne except the first-born child, who was now lost on Earth. She was a crown princess of this world, who would one day rule half the universe. However, she was unaware of this fact.

As she was growing up, an evil immortal king called Tayten came across this princess, and he wanted to train her and use her to take over the light world. Her father still had no clue that she existed. King Tayten teleported into her room one day and took her to his world. He put a magical bracelet on her that would cause her pain if she misbehaved or rose against him; with his mind, he could control her with this bracelet. King Tayten was in war with the light world, and they would try to protect the universe from this evil king.

He trained Blade in martial arts and weapons of warfare; she could fly through the universe in a spaceship, battling against her own people because she was controlled by this evil king. Her father was shocked to find out he had a daughter and realised she was under the control of this evil king. They attempted to rescue her instead of killing her, but they failed. The soldiers who came to rescue her were killed in a horrific way by the king.

King Tayten was truly evil; he would kill people by means of torment and torture, like cutting their heads off with a blunt knife and performing human sacrifices with a dagger in an occult ritual. This was the scene that Satan took over: People knelt down to this king, and mass killings would take place through the form of human sacrifices. I had no control over these scenes; they just played out in front of me. I also saw this king take my character and make her witness humans being eaten up alive by demonic creatures in an arena. He would drag my character and show her torment and even torture her.

The background story of King Tayten was that he came from Light Star and was a prince in this world, until his twin brother, King Porter, forced him to fight demonic-looking creatures with a few powerful soldiers. However, the soldiers were told to kill Prince Tayten because king Porter wanted to marry his brother's wife, Oracle, but to fulfil his wish, he needed to get rid of Prince Tayten. The soldiers surrendered him to the evil creatures and went back to their world. However, the evil creatures took him alive and predicted that he would be powerful, so they decided to keep him, tormenting him for ten years. Once he was released, Prince Tayten returned back to his world and informed his twin brother, king Porter, that the soldiers betrayed him. Not knowing that he was also betrayed by his twin brother, he ordered Prince Tayten's children into a room and killed them, placing the blame on him, using the excuse that he went insane after such torture from the demonic creatures over the ten-year period. The world and his ex-wife Oracle believed the king and sided against Prince Tayten.

They exiled him to an inescapable world, where he became sick. On his deathbed, an evil being came to Prince Tayten and offered him a deal for his soul, because he was filled with anger and wanted revenge. He sold his soul to this evil being; his eyes turned red, and he was given a power ring just like his twin brother's. This was when he became immortal. The evil being which he sold his soul to changed the world he was exiled to into a beautiful world; he named it Darkness.

He claimed revenge and tortured his brother to death, while his ex-wife Oracle committed suicide. He took half of his followers back to his world to rule over them. He infected his followers with his blood, and they turned evil and received red eyes like his. Their newborn children were also born with this evil gene and red eyes. However, these people were not immortal.

There were now two major races and two royal families, one from Darkness and the other from Light Star. King Tayten ruled over the universe until he finally lost control and Light Star recovered, separating from King Tayten and expanding their kingdom again by waging war against the kingdom of Darkness. When Tayten killed his brother, king Porter, his wife Oracle had a baby who the servants smuggled out to save the royal line. This child would have received the ring, and once Tayten lost control, the king would have returned to take his rightful place as ruler. Ten thousand years passed by when he discovered Blade on Earth and eventually ruled over her.

King Tayten was pure evil. He took advantage of my character; he raped Blade and forced her to drink blood and perform extremely evil deeds. I could feel darkness around me in this daydream world; the adrenalin pumped through my body while I interacted within this world. I would play secular music from my stereo system while I daydreamed, which enhanced my daydreaming and made it extremely addictive.

Blade was allowed to return back to Earth to live there. She could be summoned to this dark world and would open portals or touch a mirror to be transported there. My character would use a fire element as her power, and she would see people in danger and race off to save them while on Earth. King Tayten had black hair, red eyes, and a strong physique. His manner was pompous; he was in control, and no one could cross him. He was controlling and smart. He was a vampire alien who appeared as a rich gentleman with a psychopathic mindset; he wasn't the type of person to mess with. King Tayten wanted to rule the universe and claim the other powerful world under his rule. He was scary.

I was never able to come up with an ending for any of the stories. I would start again and twist a new storyline with a different view or scenario. I would initiate the story, but I never came up with the images. Each character had a different personality. My character's personality was very secretive and always tried to protect her identity. She was quiet but outspoken and was very intelligent.

This is the main storyline of my fantasy world. This world was entertaining and exciting, but it took me twenty-two years to see that this was truly Satanic. I was truly asleep and in darkness.

Just after I started to daydream, my father, siblings, and I were invited to visit my grandmother's church. A Christian man had a vision of our family and revealed to my father that we were all surrounded by flames. I was a little stunned but didn't think much of it at the time. I quickly forgot about what this man told us and didn't correct my life to what God wanted us to be. I was more concerned about daydreaming in this demonic world that Satan handed to me.

One time, Grandmother May invited this man to her house, so I decided to go there and meet him, as my grandmother lived directly behind my own house, separating us by only a gate. I became nervous because I thought God was going to reveal to him what I was doing. I didn't want to get caught and didn't want it to stop. I was happy to daydream because it entertained me, and I never wanted to give it up. God never revealed my secret to the man, but he left without asking God to deliver me. I now truly regret the mistake I made, as I could have been delivered from this condition. My family were all in serious trouble with God due to this vision, and at that time, we were not right with the Lord. Looking back now, I should have been afraid of this vision.

Being in high school didn't stop me from daydreaming. My friends talked about boys, parties, and other stuff quite often.

However, I didn't want to be involved in these types of conversations, so I escaped from reality and daydreamed instead. I was the nice quiet girl, who could hardly speak to another person without my nerves taking effect on my body. I found it hard to speak to others. I was shy and didn't have the self-confidence that my friends had. However, my life in the dream world was the opposite. I was entertaining myself constantly and didn't want to live in the real world any longer. I found an escape, and it consumed my very existence.

During high school, I went away to camp, and one night, the girls and boys came together and decided to play a game called Light as a Feather, Stiff as a Board. The teenagers all chanted the words "Light as a feather, stiff as a board" while they had one finger from each hand underneath a person's body; this person had volunteered to be the one they lifted off the ground. As they were chanting these words, they seemed to lift this person effortlessly off the ground; they all seemed to enjoy performing this.

I decided not to play, knowing something wasn't right at the time but not realising what it was. I avoided this game and learned later on in life that it was an occult game. I'm sure that Satan gave them this ability to lift a person off the ground without effort. I had been avoiding these occult games that came into my life, but I was no better off; after I avoided this game and witnessed them doing it, I turned around and returned to my daydream world instead. I was not aware that the devil had a hold on me, but I knew that it wasn't pleasing to the Lord.

In my mid-teens, I was asked to be baptised while on a conference camp at a William Branham convention. I was scared by this; deep down inside, I wasn't ready. I knew I was deep in sin, but I couldn't say no. Also, the elders of this church didn't ask us to confess our sins. After I was baptised, I thought I would attempt to stop daydreaming and leave this world behind. I did stop daydreaming for a few days, but I became agitated. I began daydreaming again on the way back home from the camp.

CHAPTER 3

ACCIDENT PRONE

IN MY LATE teens, I travelled to a country town to visit family for one week. One day, my family and I went to this waterfall area. It looked like a lagoon with rocks surrounding it and the water flowing into the lagoon from the waterfall. Some of the teenagers, including my eldest brother Paul, decided to walk up to the top of the waterfall. I ended up following them, and while we were at the top of this waterfall, Paul accidentally put his foot out, which tripped me over.

As I fell down the waterfall on my belly, I tried for dear life to grab onto something, but couldn't. The rock was completely smooth, so there was nothing to hold onto. I called upon the name of Jesus, and suddenly, I was pushed over and landed inside a deep pool, halfway down the waterfall. I know that the Lord saved me that day. Had I landed at the bottom of the waterfall, I would have certainly landed on the rocks, being seriously injured or even killed. As I climbed out of that rock pool and got to safety, I still did not repent and turn to the Lord with all my heart. I did love the Lord but couldn't give up these deep, dark sins that I kept hidden from people.

For five years, I held a nursing position at an aged-care facility. It was a hard job, and although it weighed heavily on my body, it was also a very rewarding job. Unsure of what I wanted to do after high school, I decided to complete a certificate in nursing with a close friend of mine. After completing this course, I decided to study science, completing a certificate in laboratory skills, and then commenced a diploma in laboratory technology (pathology testing). Soon after I enrolled in this programme, I happened to find the nursing job and was no longer able to study. In saying this, my heart was no longer into completing the course either, as I woke up one day and decided that science wasn't something I wanted to explore anymore.

As I looked after the patients at the aged-care facility, I met an elderly lady with schizophrenia. One time after giving her a shower, I witnessed her turning her head and telling off a few voices that she heard. She looked at me awkwardly and brushed it off. She never told me much about her experiences with these voices, but I could tell she wasn't happy when they spoke to her. Being an inexperienced nurse, I didn't know much about mental health at the time. I just thought she was hearing voices, and that was it. However, it wasn't until I went through a few things myself that I fully understood what these voices were.

I would work afternoon shifts at the aged-care facility; most of my work colleagues were young university students, studying to become registered nurses. I never thought much of what I wanted to become. Currently, I'm working as a receptionist in a chiropractic clinic. It's been a number of years since my days of working as a nurse. One day at the aged-care facility, I was challenging a colleague about evolution. She argued with me, and I spoke back regarding my beliefs. I was witnessing to her about the accuracy of the Bible and how the Lord created everything. This was the second time I witnessed to another soul; my husband Joshua was the first one I witnessed to. I was a confused mess at the time, daydreaming secretly and then witnessing to the lost souls when deep down, I was lost too.

I believed in the Lord and stood by him and fought against evolution. I even gave her a video of a creationist documentary to show her a bit about what I believed. She watched the tape but dismissed the idea and added, "I read the Bible once, and I don't believe in the blood of Jesus."

She didn't like the idea of the Lord dying on the cross and his blood being shed for her. One morning, I had a dream which left me puzzled. Unaware at the time what Satan can do within a dream, I dreamt that I was in bed with this colleague; she was a lesbian in my dream. I dismissed the dream and went to work that same day to find out that she actually was. She revealed the news to all the staff that she started to date another female nurse. Satan had given me this dream before I even found out that she was a lesbian.

My biggest fear after my mother passed away was to see a dead person. I couldn't get over the idea that I was working within a facility where people I took care of passed away on a regular basis. I praise the Lord now that within a five-year period of working there, I never once had to deal with a patient's dead body. God had kept me from it; he knew I feared this the most. People had died on my shift, but I was never the one to attend to the body.

A year before I was married, I left Joshua's place and headed for home. On the way, I fell into a micro sleep while driving and crashed the car into a telephone pole. I got out of the car with minor injuries, while the car was declared a write-off. Out of fear, I ended up lying to the police about the events of this car accident. I told them that I hit a pothole and lost control of the steering, which caused me to step on the accelerator. What a bad move on my end. I really regretted this lie and would love to remove it from my life. Before the accident, I remember I was driving the car and then just simply blanked out. As I hit the kerb, it woke me up just in time to see me hit the pole. I was stunned and just sat inside the vehicle until someone came to my rescue. I was taken to the local hospital and received a few stitches to my knee. After this event, I had the most realistic dream. In this dream, I was driving the car and experienced the car accident all over again. I woke up completely shaken by this, with a feeling like this accident was a warning call to me.

Felicity invited me, my husband, and our eldest daughter Violet to her son's first birthday party. It was raining, and the roads were wet. I happened to be at the shops when Felicity called me. She told me not to come up to the party because of the wet conditions.

However, I said, "We'll come anyway."

As I went to pay at the cash register, I took notice of the radio, which was broadcasting the weather. I found it a bit creepy and thought it felt like a warning. It got my attention, like in a movie before something happens. When I arrived home, Sally also called me. She told me that she was not going to the party any longer because of the wet conditions. She suggested that we not go either, but we dismissed her suggestion and got into the car to make the two-hour trip.

Just before driving off, I asked Joshua, "Do you think we should still go because it's wet?"

He replied, "We'll take it easy and drive up slowly."

We were only fifteen minutes away from our destination when Joshua unexpectedly lost control of the car as he drove around a large bend. We crossed two empty oncoming lanes and ploughed the boot of our car into a tree. As he lost control, time seemed to slow down. As time slowed down, two thoughts entered my mind: The first thought was, *My daughter is going to die.* The second thought was to call out to Jesus to save us, which I did. I once again used his name. In my surprise, Violet, Joshua, and I all came out alive and without a scratch. At that moment, I developed a deep fear that I was going to hell. I started to think about my eternity, but still I didn't instantly repent and turn to the Lord.

One day, Joshua played a supernaturally themed cartoon for Violet to watch. I didn't mind at the time, and I sat down with her and started to watch this cartoon. As I was watching a scene with spirits and demonic creatures, something hit me like a pile of bricks. It was God's wrath that fell over me. I panicked and immediately took the USB stick out of the television. I deleted the cartoon off it and also deleted the original file from the computer. At this stage,

I was far from the Lord. I no longer attended church or read the Bible. However, I still loved him and would tell people that I was a Christian. I couldn't deny him or the faith.

One time, Sally asked me to come back to Jesus. These words sunk deep into my heart, and I became sad. However, I couldn't come back to him because I was deep in sin by daydreaming the way I did. I was truly hurt and couldn't face him. I told her with a sad heart that I had my reasons why I couldn't come back to him. I was regretting my own words. I hated what I had just said. I could feel my tears building behind my eyes, and my throat went dry.

CHAPTER 4

WE ARE HERE

In 2014, I became annoyed with my daydreaming world; I was bored because I no longer had the ability to enter into King Tayten's kingdom within this dream state. It was like someone had put a hold on this world, enforcing it in my heart and mind not to seek after him. The storyline became boring. Instead, I stayed up and watched every supernatural television series that was out in 2014, until I came across one that made me very upset. I hated the ending, for it was far too dark and evil for me.

Angry and annoyed, I said, "That's it … I'm done!"

I decided then and there that I was no longer going to watch anything evil ever again. I sat on the couch and said, "Lord, can I come back home to you?"

I was tossing and turning; I wanted to return to the Lord but wasn't able to.

One night not long after this, I sat down and watched a documentary on television about a Christian church. The host of the show mocked the church because of their attitude towards the gay community and other issues. When they mentioned the Antichrist, I suddenly heard a voice speak to me, saying, "We are here."

The fear of the Lord God gripped me, so I immediately got on my knees and repented, turning away from all evil. I knew hearing those words caused me to repent. However, this wasn't the Holy Spirit which spoke to me, but a spirit. I believe this spirit was from the Lord.

I truly repented and turned back to God. I gave up imagining and never went back to my dream world again. I removed the stereo away from my room and placed a Bible on my bedside table where it used to sit; I no longer watched secular movies or listened to secular music. I placed my supernatural television shows, movies, secular music, and anything associated with the world in the rubbish bin (except for an expensive mask which sat in a glass cabinet). Joshua didn't allow me to throw out some of the items; I told him that they were all his, as I didn't want to be associated with these items any longer.

One day, I noticed that the Lord started giving me hymns, which just came to me. They were songs from my childhood that had been forgotten; I didn't remember them. Also, these songs were not attached to my own thoughts; they were flowing thoughts. I started to notice this and went online to look up the words to these songs. The first song that I received was "Just as I Am without One Plea," and the words touched my heart. All the songs I received gave me such hope. I started to read and listen to the Bible every day and started to pray and fast.

One morning, as I was awaking out of sleep, I heard these words: "Burdens are lifted at Calvary. Jesus is very near." I recognised that these words came from the song "Burdens Are Lifted at Calvary." The Lord was telling me he is coming soon. I was so excited and tried to prepare my life away from the world and to praise God and listen to his word every single day.

One day, I was trying to figure out who the Lord was. I still had the Jesus-only doctrines inside my head and could not admit to what the Bible was showing me about the Lord Jesus and our Father in heaven. I knew there was only one God, but I could see three which bared record in heaven. I started to cry with all my heart while I was cooking a meal for my family, telling the Lord, "I don't know you at all."

I decided to go and empty the rubbish bin; when I opened the front door, I saw the most perfect rainbow I had ever seen. It was so bright and clear. As I had opened the front door and spotted the rainbow, this incredible feeling of love and peace entered my body. In awe of such a presence, I soaked it all in and then showed my children the rainbow in excitement, explaining to them that this was a covenant the Lord gave to us to never flood the earth again.

When Violet was five, she woke up early one morning and went to the bathroom. The noise that she was making woke me up. I decided to get out of bed and check up on her. As I approached her, she then heard a sound like a shofar; She quickly told me, "Mum, I can hear a trumpet sounding like the one you showed me," referring to a lesson on the Jewish shofar, which I taught her earlier in the week.

It frightened me because it was a silent morning, and I thought that I was not ready to meet the Lord (even though I wanted the rapture to happen). It was a wake-up call for me, that I still wasn't ready to meet him.

She then slept in my bed and heard angels singing. She looked up and said, "Mum, I can hear singing."

I decided to do a fast for the Lord and ended up fasting for two days straight. On the second day of the fast, I heard a male voice say to me clearly, "Do a third day!" I now realise that it was an evil spirit pushing me to continue fasting for a third day. This demonic voice came from outside of me. I never did fast for the third day, even though I really wanted to.

While I was driving home from my daughter's school, the Lord gave me the song, "I'm So Glad Jesus Set Me Free," and I started to sing it. When I got to the verse, "Satan had me bound but Jesus set me free," a woman who was in the opposite lane looked over at me and started to abuse me.

Our windows were both up. I looked at her and wondered why she was abusing me. I didn't do anything to her that I was aware of. I just continued on singing and drove off. When I was singing this song, I did direct it to Satan, that Jesus set me free.

CHAPTER 5

DREAMS

When I first came back to the Lord, I started receiving dreams. I realise that many Christians receive dreams; some are from the Lord, and others are from Satan. Here are a few examples of what our Father in heaven, Jesus, and the devil has given me within a dream.

One night, this dream came to me: I found myself on a wide, dark road full of people. All the people were running towards their destruction. Their destination was hell. At the edge of a cliff, I saw this image of Jesus (I truly don't know if this was a false Jesus); people were picking up their bows and arrows, and releasing their arrows into the crowd. To my relief, the arrows just missed me. The dream ended, and I heard a voice, knowing full well that it was our Lord Jesus speaking to me. The Lord said, "If you hear my words and do them, you will be saved."

I had another dream where I received a boot and heard these words: "This is a covenant between you and me." I was given a box of tissues and saw a light behind the boot. I really felt like God, our Father, sent me this dream, because I had a strong feeling of God's presence when I received it. The dream felt like I was given a promise. He was telling me in a way that I was going to cry, which was true. My future became extremely hard, which you will see why.

In another dream, I was in the backyard when a plane crashed onto our house, causing it to catch on fire. In the next scene, I saw Violet on fire and quickly told her to roll on the grass to extinguish the flame. As I was saying this, the fire also landed on my face and hands. The scene changed, and I found myself arguing in the kitchen with Joshua. From this scene, I ended up in hospital and saw Jesus standing next to me. He was my doctor, and I heard him say, referring to my youngest child Ruby, "She is safe." He showed me her cot; Ruby was sound asleep in it. At the time, I didn't know what this dream meant. This dream resembled my future. The Lord had sent me a warning in advance that disaster was around the corner.

This nightmare was from Satan: I was outside in our front yard, and our small red car was parked on the lawn, like normal. I noticed I was my character Blade and felt like something was about to happen. I quickly swam out of the dream, calling on Jesus to get me out of there. I was so afraid because I knew the scene was set up for something to happen. The Lord helped me get out of this dream before anything took place.

In another dream, I was sitting in my grandmother's church. I saw a door on the left-hand side of me. It had light coming from it, and a cold wind was coming through the door. I saw a lady turn around and shiver in the cold, and the men of the church were trying to close this door. Then the scene changed as I began to hear secular music, and I asked them, "Who let this music into the church?"

They replied "The pastor did."

I saw the pastor standing at the front of the church and asked him, "Do you think you will make the rapture?"

This was when I woke up. I believe this was from the Lord. I believe all pastors should look at themselves and see if they have let too much of the world into the churches.

Another time, I dreamt I was outside in our backyard, and I had a few pieces of clothing sitting in a clothes basket, ready to hang up. I said, "By the time I hang these up, the Lord will return." This was from the Lord.

In another dream, I found myself in an elaborate room. As I stood in front of these massive doors, all of a sudden, fear gripped me. I saw how the doors shook violently, making a banging noise. Demons were behind these doors, wanting to enter through them to get to me. I was surrounded by the presence of evil, but suddenly, while in this dream state, I said, "I rebuke you in the name of Jesus." Immediately, the doors stopped banging, and I awoke out of my sleep. I realised it was God who allowed me to rebuke demons while dreaming, which left me amazed because this would be the first experience I had rebuking demons.

Another time, I dreamt I was by myself in a hotel room, and I went over to this bedside table. Right behind me appeared a white spirit, and with a loud voice, it reached out its hand and said "Come here." Fear struck me, so I shouted out, "I rebuke you in the name of Jesus," while still asleep. As I was awaking out of my sleep, I continued to repeat these words. I didn't want to go back to bed after this attack because I was so afraid, shaking from the experience.

On the news, I began to notice certain subjects highlighted, like the Hadron Collider from CERN. I felt this presence in the room as it drew me towards the television. This also happened to me while watching news converge of Israel's Prime Minister Benjamin Netanyahu, who spoke to the American Congress in 2015. At the time, I thought it was the Lord, but I now believe it came from the devil, who highlighted these events and drew me to the television and You Tube to look deeper into these things.

I became hooked on YouTube and started to search on a daily basis for prophecies from the Lord Jesus, God, disasters, and so on. I have to explain why I believed that we could receive prophecies from our Lord: It was because God poured out his spirit onto everyone, as is stated in Acts 2:17–18:

"And it shall come to pass in the last days, saith God, I will pour out of my Spirit upon all flesh: and your sons and your daughters shall prophesy, and your young men shall see visions, and your old men shall dream dreams: And on my servants and on my handmaidens I will pour out in those days of my Spirit; and they shall prophesy."

I truly believed these people, because they were claiming to be Christians, but I didn't even think about the enemy and what they had done to the church of God. Some Christians are deceived by spirits because they hear a voice and believe it's from the Lord; they are not able to discern them, like the Bible states in 1 John 4:1–3:

"Beloved, believe not every spirit, but try the spirits whether they are of God: because many false prophets are gone out into the world. Hereby know ye the Spirit of God: Every spirit that confesseth that Jesus Christ is come in the flesh is of God: And every spirit that confesseth not that Jesus Christ is come in the flesh is not of God: and this is that spirit of antichrist, whereof ye have heard that it should come; and even now already is it in the world."

I didn't understand just how much the enemy could blind us, until I went on a particular YouTube channel set up by a woman named Anne, who believed she was hearing directly from our Lord Jesus Christ.

CHAPTER 6

FALLING AWAY

ANNE APPEARED TO be a Christian and claimed to be receiving prophecies from Jesus nearly every night. I know in our Christian walk, we can talk to our God directly, and he does respond to us through our very spirit. I'll give you a few examples: He can wake us up to go into prayer or to spend time with him before going off to a busy schedule. He can remind us of important things that we would forget otherwise. He can rebuke us if we step out of his will. This can happen several times a day; I've experience this first-hand. The Lord can speak directly through our mouth or even directly to us. Other times, we need to seek the Lord earnestly with prayer, sometimes for hours on end. We also need to make sure that we are not deceived by an evil spirit. We need to discern who we are talking to. We do this by testing the spirits. However, the way Anne received her prophecies was through prayer. The Lord recently opened my eyes to the demon behind her messages. Anne would claim that this Jesus would come and spend time with her nearly every single night. Anne would then record the conversation she had with this spirit which claimed to be Jesus. Anne sounded like a genuine Christian; however, when you look deep into her doctrines and prophecies that she has posted up on her channel, you can see that they are completely false and unbiblical.

Unless God pulls you out of such a situation or you test the spirits to get an answer, you are trapped and serving the devil. Even if this person is told that they are receiving their prophecies from a demon, they won't believe you because they are hearing a voice and truly believe it is from the Lord.

When I went on her channel, I instantly fell away from the truth and fell asleep. My eyes became closed, and I was blinded by this false Jesus. For the first time in my life, I was drawn away from the true Jesus Christ.

I can now see how Christians are deceived by these channels. Those who are on such channels believe that these prophecies are coming from the Lord, but they are really receiving false prophecies from unclean spirits and doctrines taught by demons. I'm not saying every channel isn't from the Lord, and Christians do post up true messages from God. However, this particular channel was not from the Lord. Out of legal reasons, I'm not able to name and shame this channel.

"Now the Spirit speaketh expressly, that in the latter times some shall depart from the faith, giving heed to seducing spirits, and doctrines of devils." (1 Timothy 4:1)

It all began when I was searching YouTube and accidently ended up in the middle of one of her videos clips. I automatically heard a third person in her message and was drawn towards it. This third person was a demon which gave her these messages. I heard the message and imagined a male voice loud and clear coming from her. My eyes twinkled away, and I was lost from that moment on. "Ice skating on Saturn with the Lord Jesus," I heard her say through her message. Addiction set in, and I started to crave her messages every single day. Anne spoke a lot about the bride of Christ and marrying Jesus. She even had a detailed vision of her marrying the Lord Jesus and has also published a so-called Christian book regarding her experiences with this spirit. I want to explain that Satan can give you a vision.

As I viewed her videos, Satan and the devils attempted to brainwash me by using her information. This was the beginning of a battle which erupted between Satan, the demons, and me. I was so ignorant about demons that I wasn't even aware of what they were about to do to me until I experienced it.

Unaware that Satan had just entrapped me again with this channel, I began to experience the supernatural on a whole new level.

I was at home one day when my heart felt as if it was crushed into pieces. I was in agony and crying out in pain. A thought had entered my mind, telling me that Jesus had just broken my heart, like a boyfriend crushing his girlfriend's heart when they break up. I didn't understand that I was being attacked spiritually. I could see this occurring, but nothing registered inside of me that demons started to attack me.

Another evening, I decided to lie down on the couch, and this feeling of bliss came upon me. A tingling feeling entered my heart and spread throughout my body. I was on a blissful drug of pure bliss, and it felt incredible. I started to want this feeling and would seek it out on a daily basis; it would come to me and take me away into a state of pure bliss again and again. I didn't even realise who was behind this experience, as I lay there patiently waiting for this to happen. It was so pleasant, and I really enjoyed it. I was lured away by it.

"I am floating away," I told my sister Sally while on the phone to her.

She asked me, "Are you okay?"

I was all high from the experience and mumbled away a few other things to her. I didn't specify anything else to her, nor did I mention that I was constantly on this channel. I kept it as a secret. I felt something telling me that it was wrong to be on this channel. However, I didn't pay attention to this warning.

One evening, I was in my room, wide awake, when Satan dragged me into the dream world. I didn't enter willingly. I found myself in this large room and saw this person playing a grand piano; the music he played intrigued me. Who was this person playing the piano? I didn't imagine any of the scenes. I was taken deep into the spirit world in a moment of time. As I was viewing this scene, I suddenly fell asleep.

Another time, while I was watching one of her videos, my eyes were suddenly opened to the dream world. The scene was about the bride of Christ gathering together in heaven. However, this wasn't from the Lord but from Satan.

I watched a video clip she promoted of a man teaching people how to hear the voice of God. As I clicked on the clip, he said to just listen to the voice instead of your head. This is what I picked up on from this teaching. I got into the shower and meditated on my thoughts; I searched inside my mind for a voice from the Lord. All of a sudden, I heard male demonic voices all yelling inside my mind. I know now it wasn't my own thoughts but spirits. I was completely wrong to look inside my mind. You cannot hear from the Lord like this. The Lord told me one day that none of this man's teachings were from the Lord. You will most likely come across a devil by doing this and not find the Lord's voice this way. I would love to name these people; however, out of legal reasons, I can't.

This happened to me before I had a deep and personal relationship with God. Please be aware of such teachings and do not search your mind like I did for the voice of the Lord. These demonic voices stopped and disappeared on me. After hearing the demonic yelling of voices that came from inside my mind, I opened the front door and went outside my house; I looked up at the moon and wondered how beautiful God's creation was, when I heard a subtle whisper inside my mind. A voice just spoke to me, but no one was there. This was an evil spirit which came to me and whispered something inside my mind.

This demon came to me gradually over a two-month period, and it started portraying to me to be our Lord Jesus Christ. He was luring me over to him by pretending to be Jesus. I don't know why to this day I fell for it. He was trying to win me over by communicating with me about being one of his brides. I became brainwashed and started to listen to him.

At this stage, I could feel the presence of demons inside my house. I felt surrounded by torment, and it was putting severe pain throughout my entire body. The more and more I visited Anne's channel, the more deluded I became. I thought that I had found the Lord.

At around this time, I went into our lounge room and saw Satan. He stood opposite me, and I started to resist him like the Bible teaches. I referred to this verse:

"Wherefore take unto you the whole armour of God, that ye may be able to withstand in the evil day, and having done all, to stand." (Ephesians 6.13)

I know now it wasn't Satan himself but a visual of him that was portrayed in my imagination. I had no control over what was shown to me, neither did I think him up. I resisted, and he then disappeared. I was so happy; I thought I won. I quickly decided to praise the Lord by playing a Christian anthem. I was dancing around, praising and singing to God, when all of a sudden, an invisible spirit entered my house. This evil spirit stood in front of me and then quickly grabbed me in reality and danced a waltz with me to this beat. I ended up dancing with it and became overwhelmed by the experience. The spirit then knocked me into the kitchen wall and continued dancing with me. It then entered my body; it spoke through me and said, "I am the queen of heaven," and other crazy and evil stuff. It's strange because this spirit was invisible, but I could still see this demon and feel his presence.

I saw this spirit as an invisible human man, presenting itself as romantic and alluring. This was the way it portrayed itself to me, as it grabbed my hands and gently and forcefully danced this waltz with me. I completely forgot who I was as I danced with evil and was enjoying the experience at the same time. I really regret this now with tears. I really didn't understand what came over me.

One morning, I visited a website that promoted the serpent seed. This person wrote in graphic detail what he believed the serpent did to Eve, and as soon as I started to read this, a spirit entered my body and started giving me a strong sexual desire. I resisted while I sat at the computer, still reading the text. I wasn't sure what was happening. It was trying to give me an orgasm while trying to pervert me towards this doctrine. The author wrote a detailed story of the serpent sleeping with Eve sexually, and the spirit took advantage of me; it wanted me to accept this sexual desire. I didn't have a say in what was happening to me. I just had to resist this; however, I was so overwhelmed by it that I couldn't think straight. I didn't pray or rebuke it in the name of Jesus. I just sat there, completely resisting this supernatural urge. It stunned me that the spirit was able to do this with such force. After I resisted the spirit, it quickly left.

I found a binding prayer on Anne's channel. I said, "I'm going to pray this five times a day because it's not hard to pray." It referred to unidentified flying objects and binding the enemy from all witchcraft and evil curses, things like this. I started to read the prayer and over time began to say it in a very evil way. I spoke out this prayer almost like I was casting a spell, not praying. While I was praying this and being on Anne's channel, I started to see UFOs around.

Before I go into what happened to me, I want to share a few testimonies that I've watched of Christians who have had encounters with alien beings. One time, a Christian man lay paralysed in his bedroom when these alien beings entered into his house. He could only use his mind, so he called out Jesus using his thoughts. These beings fled instantly, delivering him from further abductions. Another time, a lady used the name of Jesus, and an angel rescued her from the alien beings that entered her house. I've used the name of Jesus many times when I had trouble. His name was one of the first things that entered my mind. His name is powerful, and we as Christians can and should use it.

Another interesting testimony that I came across was of a woman who called out to Jesus for help during an alien encounter. These beings entered into her house, and they instantly fled when she called out to Jesus. Sometime after the attack, the Lord Jesus spoke to her and told her that these alien beings she had encountered were actually demons.

I was driving the car to my daughter's school in order to pick her up, and Joshua came with me, when I was unsuspectingly drawn to look up into the sky. As I looked up, I clearly saw two circular reflective discs in a diagonal line. These discs disappeared right in front of my eyes. I then saw them reappear.

I quickly said to Joshua, "Look! There are UFOs outside the car," pointing at them.

He missed it.

The reflective discs appeared another day while I was in the backyard. I was sitting outside on the steps of the trampoline and just looked up and saw them. I saw two reflective unidentified flying objects in a diagonal line. I told Violet to look up, but it was too late, as they were gone. She never saw them.

On another day, I was at home taking photos when I was again drawn outside to the backyard. I had the camera in my hand; at the time, I thought that the Lord took me outside. However, I know now it was a spirit. I took a photo of this image from my camera. This thing had a round circular shape with a massive red tail following behind it. I saw it in the distance; it stopped in mid-air and then descended slowly behind the house, out of my view.

On a different night, I again took the camera outside and asked the Lord if he could show me another unidentified flying object, just like the ones I had seen. I know now that I should have never asked the Lord for this. All of a sudden, as I was looking at the night sky and the stars, I felt this searing pain running through my body. Something hit me from behind, so I turned around to see what it was, and all of a sudden, out of nowhere, this starlike object flashed out of sight in the blink of an eye. It just disappeared. It was another UFO. I went inside and didn't tell anyone what had just happened to me.

I was invited to a wedding with Joshua. I felt sick, and to make it worse, I was attacked by spirits. They were all around me; they made me feel dizzy and almost faint. I could hardly stand up on my feet from all the attacks I received that day. I struggled to get ready. For some reason, I couldn't comprehend that demons were attacking me. We dropped the children off at my in-laws' place, and Joshua and I drove off to the wedding. As we were driving, I noticed a pillar of fire burning from the corner of my eye. This pillar of fire was high in the sky, far away in the distance. I didn't mention this to my husband but just kept on staring at this in amazement. I didn't know what it was, but I knew it was supernatural in appearance. Shortly after we arrived at the wedding, the entertainment commenced. It was a modern hip-hop routine. I was stunned by the evil which surrounded me and felt the presence of evil inside that room. I couldn't take it at all. I had to walk outside of the room. I mostly stayed outside of the room, unable to take the secular music and the atmosphere that came with it. When the wedding reception came to an end, I was keen to get back home.

One mid-afternoon, I decided to take a bath. I was trying to relax and decided to start my imagination up again. Anne said that she would dance with the Lord Jesus in a vision that she had. Yes, dance with Jesus in a vision! This is how a demon can operate. Satan's agenda is to fool everyone, and he can do it in a very drastic way. Unfortunately, Anne will never believe the truth because she is deceived by this demon. All she has to do is ask this spirit if the Lord came in the flesh. While in the bathroom, I started to imagine a scene like I used to in my daydream world. Being completely relaxed in a meditated state, this world instantly opened up again. I let the enemy in and started imagining my character having fun, racing under the sea. While I was in this state, I was suddenly taken to a ship, where I sat next to an image of Jesus and played with the water, sitting next to him. I didn't come up with the ship or the image of Jesus; they just appeared without me thinking about it. This Jesus was from Satan.

I got out of the bathtub, and again a demon affected my heart in the supernatural. I was in so much pain, I cried out in tears. I grabbed the iPad and sat down as I listened to a hymn named "Be Thou My Vision," while I cried my heart out to God. As I was crying, I felt my heart heal supernaturally. I know it was God who healed me, who picked up all the broken pieces and put my heart back together. This was truly the Lord's work; even though I fell away from the truth, in that moment, I put my trust in him, and he healed me.

I instantly felt better, but instead of realising I was being attacked by demons and only turn to the Lord, I went back to this channel and watched another video. I was addicted to this male voice which revealed himself through the messages that she delivered.

As I started to search Anne's videos, I came across one which showed me how to meditate with meditation music. I thought I would do this, and as I listened to her voice, I imagined sitting on a bridge. Suddenly, I saw an image of Jesus walk up to me as I sat on this bridge. We decided to walk off the bridge, and the scene then took me and this Jesus to a beach. I played in the sand and made a sandcastle, placing diamond love hearts on top of the sandcastle. As I was doing this, I was having a conversation with this Jesus figure. I told him, "I am heartbroken and upset." Somehow, I was comforted by this experience. It's strange because I knew not to meditate before I fell away, but I went blind and didn't understand that I was meditating, even though I knew I was. You shouldn't meditate this way. Be careful of any forms of meditation, as we should only meditate on the word of God. The enemy got to me during meditation.

Also, the demons kept on trying to sexually pervert me towards the Lord Jesus. However, I only saw Jesus Christ as my saviour. I never truly fell for this woman's teachings concerning Jesus being my real husband or being one of his real brides. I continued to question this. I believe that the saints of God are the bride of Christ. When I listened to these messages, for some strange reason, nothing registered within my brain that this was false. Every sound doctrine which I knew of previously began to escape my mind. I had filled it with false messages from a demon. Over time, the false Jesus who surrounded me twisted my mind, which caused me to fall for a few of her doctrines.

I started dreaming in a very perverse way at this time. I had these dreams where I dreamt that I was holding hands with a false Jesus. This Jesus was the same image from the ship and meditation. He showed me that he was giving me baby pink wedding flowers. I also dreamt that I was writing in a journal, and I had the false Jesus sit next to me, like I was in a romantic position with him. He tried to correct my writing by saying, "What are you writing here?" in a gentle manner. I woke up confused by these dreams. This is how the enemy works. They plant these types of dreams to lure you away into sin and deception. Satan can even use other types of dreams to get you to desire another person or put hatred in your heart towards others. Satan tried to do this to me several times throughout my life.

Another day, I was at home when a demon entered me. I felt this strong supernatural desire hit me hard. I was forced to the ground and lay still, resisting the urge to have an orgasm. I didn't understand at the time that I was wrestling with a spirit. The sexual pressure grew more and more, until it finally gave up and left my body. I fought hard against it and never gave up. I didn't want what Satan was offering me. They were forcing me to accept this, but I refused.

I was resting on my bed when I got attacked again. The sexual urge rushed through my private parts, and I started to resist it. This was the third time it had happened, but this time, it was different. The spirit started telling me in a silent way that he was the Lord Jesus and to have this with him. Perversion set in, and I dashed into the shower; I quickly undressed and sat on the ground, as I resisted it with the water running over me. After a few minutes, it left me once again.

One night, I was waiting for Joshua to get ready, as we were all going out for dinner. I decided to get the children into the car; they were ready to go. The moon was perfect that night, and there was a peaceful stillness in the night air. I couldn't understand what it was, but it felt supernatural, and I took note of it. We went out to dinner with my husband's family and then returned home. Joshua headed off to work, and I put the children to sleep and lay down in my bed.

I heard these words reach me: "I am going to stop the great tribulation and rapture you." I was told this by a demon portraying itself as Jesus. He then alarmed me and yelled in a panic, "I am coming now!"

I jumped out of bed and went into the kitchen. Suddenly, the demon spoke again and told a few demons who were masquerading as angels to take me back to my bed. I felt a spirit pull me along until I reached my room. As I climbed into bed, I felt a horde of demons hit me like a ferocious wind and with such force that I thought I was going to die. They put me through such absolute fear that I passed out. It was one of the worst experiences I have ever had. It was meant to kill me, and I believe if it wasn't for the Lord, I would have died out of fear. For some reason, the Lord didn't want me to die that night.

A demon tugged at my body, which pulled me out of my slumber. I arose out of bed and forgot that I had been demonically attacked just hours earlier. I acted as if nothing had happened to me. It was around 4 a.m. when I decided to turn on the computer. I wanted to play a popular Christian song. The lyrics talked about the dawn, and I suddenly had a thought enter my mind: *The rapture is going to happen this morning.*

Convinced by the lyrics and my own messed-up thoughts, I opened the roman blinds and stepped outside into the backyard. I looked about aimlessly at the darkened morning sky and saw the stars twinkling high above my head. They were all beautiful, and I marvelled at them all.

I walked over to the trampoline and took a seat just above the steps. The darkened sky started to fade away, and the stars began to disappear out of my view. I saw the most perfect morning that day. It was peaceful, there were birds flying by, and I marvelled in awe at the most perfect scene. *Dawn was approaching,* I thought. Then I heard a voice start to speak to me. It was the false Jesus spirit. We started a two-way conversation again in which it told me I wasn't allowed to go back inside the house, or the Great Tribulation would still occur. I thought I would be the one to help stop all the upcoming disasters that the tribulation would bring, but at this point in my life, my view of the Bible was extremely twisted. Anne's channel had warped my mind with false doctrines and demonic messages.

I ate into every word this spirit told me. He continued, "We will have a honeymoon together in heaven for seven years. We will then come back to Earth to rule together."

I started to cry with all my heart, thinking I didn't want to go without my children. I couldn't imagine missing out on their lives for seven years. Suddenly, from out of nowhere, the sun appeared in the sky. Thinking it was the dawn, I waited in excitement for the rapture to happen. The sun was still in front of my eyes and was not rising. I waited and waited, but nothing happened. I had just experienced a vision from the devil which fooled me completely and left me wondering.

I heard a set of keys jingling together from the backyard. Somebody was opening the front door. It was Joshua. He had just come home from working a long overnight shift. I remembered the spirit's words about not going inside, but I was tired and decided to risk it. I made a cup of coffee for the both of us and started to panic a little as I realised I had just witnessed the sun standing still. I went online and looked up the latest news articles to see if there had been any reports on such a massive event. There was nothing on the news, and no one reported anything on the sun. I became fearful and started longing to escape to get away from it all. We had a holiday booked, and I was relieved that we were going away.

CHAPTER 7

THE HOLIDAY

PACKING OUR BAGS was a challenge. The false Jesus was helping me pack our bags. He said, "Just take this many; that's enough clothes for the week." He was actually helping me but also stopping me from packing. At this stage, I was a mess. I lost every sense of soundness that I thought I once had.

It was 1 a.m. the morning that we were leaving to go on holidays. I had finished packing our bags when I heard bird sounds coming from the bathroom. It made me feel like I was trapped inside my mind. I started to touch the white tiles of the bathroom and then began to push at them. I started telling myself, "This reality can't be real." I believed this lie.

I went into our bedroom, confused by all of it, and sat down on the floor, leaning against the wall. A voice suddenly broke through the air. God was calling me (so I thought). He wanted to pull me out of this trapped reality. He told me I was a one-hundred-year-old lady who was dying and had been trapped in my mind for years. This was an evil spirit that started to destroy me.

I sat on the ground, accepting this fact, when my mind suddenly veered over to my children and husband, assuming they weren't real. I tried to die and let go but couldn't. This demon hit me hard with the most diabolical lie I had ever seen, and I had fallen right into its trap. I gave up trying to die and climbed back into bed. The demon made me think that I went crazy.

When I awoke in the morning, I walked out to the front yard and saw the beautiful flowers.

I said, "The flowers are too beautiful; my daydream world wasn't as realistic. The Earth was too detailed; this had to be the real world."

This brought me back to reality. I was not trapped in my mind. Accepting this fact, I started to become extremely fearful and had to leave the demons behind. Around this time, I did and didn't know that I had demons attacking me, for fear and delusion played a large toll on my mind.

As I ran away from the house, scared and relieved, thinking that I could escape the torment and go on holidays, the evil spirit appeared to me again. It was trying to comfort me on the shuttle bus to the airport. He kept repeating these words: "It's okay," and "It'll be okay." A tormenting feeling came over me. I leant on the window, listening to this sound all the way to the airport. As I got to the airport, the false Jesus told me to write a letter to this YouTube channel and try and stop it, because it wasn't from God. "When I get back, I'll stop the channel," I replied.

Even with the spirit telling me the truth, I still couldn't wake up from being completely deluded and blind.

We boarded the plane, and it took off. Everything seemed to go back to normal; however, I was extremely tired and wanted to sleep, but couldn't. Ruby was on my lap, and Violet was in the seat next to me. Joshua fell asleep as soon as he sat down. Just before the plane was due to land, a voice suddenly broke the air, instantly attracting my attention. It was meant to be God. It spoke out quickly, looking for me, and then disappeared, leaving me in absolute fear. The demon made me feel as if I was trapped inside my mind once again. I became nervous, quiet, and still. I began to reconsider my life, pondering that I was indeed trapped inside my mind and not actually living in the real world any longer.

As the plane landed at our destination, it seemed to shake violently. I sat in the seat of the plane, stunned by this, but no one else seemed to be affected by it except me. The non-realistic feeling came over me yet again, making me believe that I was trapped again. I had just eaten into a lie from Satan. It might sound like nothing, but if you heard this and experienced something like this, you would believe the lie also. It was designed in such a way to make me think that I was truly trapped inside my mind. At that moment, I really thought I was; it felt as if I was truly alone in this make-believe world.

I got out of my seat, grabbed our hand luggage, and disembarked the plane. I asked Joshua to let me go to the bathroom at the airport terminal, and Violet followed me there. I saw her at the sink, washing her hands, and the next moment, she disappeared from my vision and then reappeared instantly, right in front of my eyes. I thought I was still trapped, so I didn't panic. I was walking around in a daze with this idea that Satan put inside my head.

We were picked up by a shuttle bus which drove us to the car rental office in order to pick up our hired car. The evil spirit claiming to be God spoke to me again; he told me that I was stuck in a make-believe world that I created, and he wanted to pull me out of it. He also told me that I was the most talented person for making up such a world and that he wanted to use me to create other worlds with him.

"I want to stay until my holiday is over," I replied. "Give me a week."

I really wanted to go to Morton Bay island and walk on the beach with my kids. A beautiful image came to mind: I was walking along the beach and watching the sunset with my kids and husband. It gave me this peace. We then drove off to our hotel, stopping at a local shopping centre on the way. The shopping centre was about ten minutes away from our apartment, and we decided to let our kids play in an indoor playground. I bought a cake and coffee for me and Joshua and sat there as we looked on at the children. We needed to buy groceries for our apartment, and once again I was attacked by demons. Joshua didn't notice anything strange, as I kept it all to myself, trying to protect him and my family from Satan.

We finished shopping, packed our groceries into the car, and drove off. As I stared at the setting sun, a thought came into my mind that I was stopping the sun from setting. I still believed I was trapped inside my world that I created and thought I was able to control the scenes around me. I had a deluded feeling of peace run through my mind at this stage. We arrived at the check-in counter and went upstairs to our apartment on the fourth floor.

We unpacked everything and decided to stay in for the night, feeding the children and putting them to bed. I decided to go and have a bath. As I relaxed in the bathtub, with the water filled to the brim, my children woke up, opened the bathroom door, and walked in. I saw them both at the edge of the bathtub, and then they disappeared out of my view and re-appeared as quickly as they left.

I was shocked and made a fearful noise. Fear gripped me, and a thought entered my mind: *My children are demons.*

They walked out, and my reality shifted. I thought I went to hell. I saw the old floor tiles of the bathroom almost come alive; it was a haunting scene. I was reminded that Joshua and I died in the car accident we were involved in. We didn't survive it, and Violet went to heaven, but we ended up in hell. I pleaded to this false Jesus to come and rescue me. I heard the false Jesus tell me that he was going to rescue me from this place. He continued to say that Joshua was going to walk inside the bathroom, grab a knife, and kill me in a very horrific way, and then the scene would play all over again. That's when the false Jesus would rescue me. This spirit made it seem that this was to be the routine that was held in hell.

Joshua suddenly entered into the bathroom. I was closing my eyes when he started to call my name, "Danica, Danica," shaking me to get my attention.

My eyes and face were almost under the water; I thought, *He's about to kill me!* I tried my hardest to bear what was about to take place, submitting to it in fear. He continued to call my name and shook me; I finally opened my eyes and sat up. Joshua was just trying to snap me out of it. He had no knife, and it was all a lie. I now wonder why he came into the bathroom in the first place. It was odd that he did at that exact moment of time. The hell scene disappeared out of my mind, so I got out of the bath and didn't mention a word to him of what had just happened to me. From that point on, he started to realise something wasn't quite right with me.

Joshua went back to bed. However, I was wide awake and couldn't sleep. A demon entered the room, an evil presence that I just couldn't shake off. I felt torment and absolute fear around me. As it approached me, I felt this fear tingle inside my body. Alarmed by it, I sat up all night long in a chair. When it hit the early hours of the morning, a thought came inside my mind. The devil gave me this thought: "I rebuke you in the name of Jesus Christ sharply." I was truly trying to fight this demon but didn't know how. As I was repeating these words, another thought entered my mind: The demons were trying to force me to blaspheme God. I had to resist this thought and rebuked it immediately. As the sun rose, I felt the torment and fear flee away as this demon left.

Joshua and the children woke up around 7 a.m. I was making breakfast for them when I started to talk to this false Jesus again. I laughed and carried on, forgetting the ordeal I had just experienced. The worst thing happened to me, as the thought of Violet being a demon re-entered my mind. I became annoyed at her with every little gesture she made and started to overly discipline her because of it. My love for her started to turn to anger because of the false reality I saw in her.

I got the ironing board out and started ironing Joshua's shirt. As he put the shirt on, I saw a pentagram marked onto his shirt and quickly tried to make him take it off. When he saw the shirt, he complained and said, "You ruined my shirt." He didn't see the pentagram but only the iron marks. I took it away and tried to hide it because it was satanic, and I wanted to protect him. I was concerned with him wearing this. He then grabbed another shirt from the room and put it on instead.

We had plans to visit an amusement park that day. I was approached by a demon; it came up to me and said, "If you go to this amusement park, your children will die on the rides."

I was afraid of this, so I told Joshua that I was sick and that we couldn't go today. I locked myself in the bathroom with Ruby. Joshua was upset with me and stood at the door, trying to find out what was wrong with me. I convinced him that I was going to rest on the bed with Ruby because I wasn't well.

As I locked myself in the bathroom, I continued hearing many voices, which were all tormenting me. These voices were demon spirits. My husband thought I was just sick and left the apartment upset; he went out to lunch with Violet. The false Jesus told me that he was about to come and rapture me, and when he came, the Earth would burn. I was scared to witness this event, so I stayed in the bathroom for a couple of hours.

As time passed by, I took the risk of leaving the bathroom. I asked God two things. The first thing I said was, "Please shred me." I was in so much agony, I wanted to die. The other thing I asked God was to touch my heart and to feel the pain that I was in. I then called Joshua on the phone and apologised to him about ruining the day. We talked, and he told me he still wanted to go out, and I agreed to this. He arrived back to the apartment, and we left the building with the children.

My children, Joshua, and I rode on a vehicle that allowed you to go sight-seeing. We bought last-minute tickets, and there were four empty chairs waiting for our family. The entire vehicle was booked out for that session. *What a weird thing*, I thought. *Four empty chairs for us.* As we took our seats and drove off, the false Jesus started up a conversation with me. During the ride, my reality shifted, and I started to believe the vehicle was full of witches, warlocks, and government spies. I looked at Violet, and the thought of her being a demon child was still fresh in my mind. I became annoyed at her again, and as I saw the host of the tour hovering around Violet, I kept telling her to leave my child alone, thinking the host was trying to pass on witchcraft objects to her. She wanted to give Violet a few stickers or something of the kind, but I thought she was giving her occult objects to perform spells. The way Violet was acting was encouraging my thinking. Satan tried to put hatred in my heart towards her. I could feel it. I found that I lost a lot of love for her due to this experience. However, thanks to the Lord, I've gained it back and love her even more now. This is what Satan had placed inside my head.

When I left the house to go on holidays, I decided at the last minute to take the Bible in my handbag and leave the binding prayer at home. I made a quick decision not to take the binding prayer, due to the fact that I sensed it wasn't from the Lord.

After the tour, we went into a shopping centre. I saw the sign of a shop change into the word "CERN" right in front of my eyes. All the toys were shown to me to be deceitful. I felt like my eyes were open by the devil, and I was shown this. While walking around, I felt this evil spirit lifting up my skirt in public; I had to keep pulling my skirt back down. I was becoming annoyed and stressed by it, and wanted to return to our apartment.

The reason why Satan showed me the word "CERN" was because of all the You Tube sites that I visited. Many Christians are concerned about what CERN is researching. Some Christians have posted up video clips of how fallen angels are going to re-enter the earth through CERN's technology. They believe that this is the bottomless pit/Abyss. Let me explain what CERN's is researching. I will quote from CERN's official website.

"At CERN, the European Organization for Nuclear Research, physicists and engineers are probing the fundamental structure of the universe. They use the world's largest and most complex scientific instruments to study the basic constituents of matter – the fundamental particles. The particles are made to collide together at close to the speed of light. The process gives the physicists clues about how the particles interact, and provides insights into the fundamental laws of nature. The instruments used at CERN are purpose-built particle accelerators and detectors. Accelerators boost beams of particles to high energies before the beams are made to collide with each other or with stationary targets. Detectors observe and record the results of these collisions."

I believe the Lord is in control of everything and we don't have to fear these things. Put all your fears into the Lord hands. He will take away your burdens and fill you with joy.

We arrived back at our apartment, and as we opened the door, I saw this middle-aged woman with blonde hair sitting on the hotel chair. In an instant, she vanished into thin air. I panicked as I felt a shock run through my body. I thought this woman was a witch and that Violet was working with her to attack me, being a demon child in my delusion. I believed this woman was a demon that manifested itself to me.

In fear and terror, I quickly searched the website on my iPhone for the binding prayer from Anne's YouTube channel. I should have turned to the Bible or prayed on my knees to the Lord, but because of fear and terror, I didn't. Panicking, I looked it up and let it play. Joshua became annoyed and complained that I was on this channel again. He asked me not to go on it while we were on holidays. I should have listened, but because of all the torment, I had this feeling of constant fear that hit me hard. I couldn't shake it off. My peace was taken away from me.

The fear left me, and another reality shift happened to me. As I was in the kitchen, I thought Satan entered into Joshua. It felt that real. Joshua started to talk to me, so in fear, I began to sing "In the Name of Jesus."

Joshua constantly told me to stop, as he had enough of hearing this song. I took Ruby out of his arms. In fear of him, I told him, "This is not your child, she is my child."

I hurried to the main room and tried to lock the door behind me, but Joshua, who I thought was possessed by the devil, followed me and confronted me.

I continued avoiding him and asking him to leave me alone. As the scene kept changing, I thought now that Joshua was actually Satan; I was married to him, and the place we were staying in was Satan's kingdom in hell. There was an eerie feeling around me, and I felt evil. I thought I was trapped in hell, like it was another world, and that my children were both demons. Satan had altered my reality, and I believed a lie. When this reality shift happened, it was so subtle that you couldn't pick up on what the true perception of reality was. My perception on what appeared real was just slightly altered. This alteration was just enough to make me strongly believe in the lie that Satan was showing me.

I told Joshua to leave and take Violet with him. I quickly went outside onto the balcony, scared out of my mind, and I sat in a chair, waiting for him to pack his belongings and leave the apartment. The false Jesus appeared again and told me he was coming to rescue me from hell. I saw the moonlight appear supernaturally on the balcony, and it shone with a silver light, making me strongly believe the lie. It felt like it was a confirmation, something solid that it was going to happen for sure.

The spirit told me, "You're leaving your husband; what's the worst that could happen?" He then added, "The police and media will arrive; be ready for it."

I sat outside with Ruby on the balcony. Joshua came out because I had Ruby in my arms, not willing to let her go. I yelled at him in fear and started to sing, "In the Name of Jesus." He was concerned with my behaviour and called his family for help. He left the balcony, took Violet with him, and contacted the police.

I continued to sing "In the Name of Jesus" for a few hours straight, not stopping to take a rest. I was in absolute fear over the situation. The words to this song are as follows:

"In the name of Jesus, in the name of Jesus, we have the victory,
In the name of Jesus, in the name of Jesus, demons will have to flee."

Three police officers confronted me and covered me. I continued singing, thinking they were demons (again, this perception of reality was shown to me) and if I had stopped singing, I wouldn't be rescued by the Lord. I would be lost in hell forever. I was holding onto my daughter, trying to get us both out of hell, waiting for the Lord to rescue us this time.

The police snatched Ruby out of my hands and wrestled me to the ground. As the ambulance officers gave me an injection to put me to sleep, I got a glimpse of the police officer handing Ruby to my husband, who I still thought was Satan. It killed me inside. I fought back with all my strength but failed. It was a nightmare experience, a moment of time that you just cannot understand. I thought my child was doomed because I let her go. I just went through severe trauma, and it affected me seriously.

I woke up in a local hospital. I forgot that I even had children or a husband. I didn't know who I was exactly. I saw someone guarding me at the hospital. Suddenly, a demon said in a booming male voice, "Repent!" I thought it was God, our Father, so I said "Repent, repent, repent!"

He also told me to say, "CERN, Hadron Collider, fallen angels are going to re-enter the Earth," so I yelled out those words. Everyone in the hospital ward heard me. I was referring to YouTube and all the videos I watched on fallen angels and the Hadron Collider. I was scared to be saying this, but thought I was doing people a favour because I wanted to warn them. It just made me look insane to the doctors and hospital staff.

Since we are on this topic, I want to explain an event that is coming to the Earth which is written in the Bible called "the Day of the Lord." I will tell you an interesting testimony which God did regarding this study. One day, I was sound asleep when I heard an alarm clock sounding. God our Father woke me from my sleep with this sound. It was not my alarm clock, but a supernatural sound that came to me. You see, I had just written the below information regarding the Day of the Lord a few days before and wanted to go back and add it in the book, but I was not sure if I should. However, the Lord decided that he wanted me to add this to my book. As I awoke, he pointed to a spot within my book where he wanted me to insert my information. I immediately got up and added this information to my book at the point where God directed me to. I knew it was the Lord, and this is the information which God wanted me to reveal.

A day is coming when mankind will face one of the most horrific times in history. This day is called the Day of the Lord. God's wrath on humankind will be unleashed due to iniquity and evil done in this world. Like in the days of Noah, the ungodly will be destroyed from the Earth in the time of the Lord's wrath.

Jesus is the only door to salvation, and there is no other way to God but through him. People need to repent and seek God; you are never promised tomorrow.

"And I will punish the world for their evil, and the wicked for their iniquity; and I will cause the arrogancy of the proud to cease, and will lay low the haughtiness of the terrible." (Isaiah 13:11)

"Near is the great day of the LORD, Near and coming very quickly; Listen, the day of the LORD! In it the warrior cries out bitterly. A day of wrath is that day, A day of trouble and distress, A day of destruction and desolation, A day of darkness and gloom, A day of clouds and thick darkness, A day of trumpet and battle cry Against the fortified cities And the high corner towers. I will bring distress on men So that they will walk like the blind, Because they have sinned against the LORD; And their blood will be poured out like dust And their flesh like dung. Neither their silver nor their gold will be able to deliver them On the day of the LORD'S wrath; And all the earth will be devoured In the fire of His jealousy, For He will make a complete end, Indeed a terrifying one, Of all the inhabitants of the earth." (Zephaniah 1:14–18)

When the day of the Lord comes, a supernatural army of locusts will rise out from the bottomless pit, along with two other supernatural disasters/plagues. I will only discuss the supernatural locust army. Read Revelation 9 from the Bible to receive more information regarding this study.

Let us start with Abaddon/Apollyon, the destroyer. Who is he exactly?

The destroyer, or Abaddon/Apollyon, is an angel who is locked in the bottomless pit. I believe the bottomless pit is hell. He will be the king of a great army, which is depicted as the locust army. This king (the destroyer) is not Satan! This army is depicted as locusts because they are vast in number and strength, and they devour everything in their path.

"And they had a king over them, which is the angel of the bottomless pit, whose name in the Hebrew tongue is Abaddon, but in the Greek tongue hath his name Apollyon." (Revelation 9:11)

When the day of the Lord arrives, an angel falls from heaven and opens the door to the bottomless pit, releasing this army upon the Earth.

"And the fifth angel sounded, and I saw a star fall from heaven unto the earth: and to him was given the key of the bottomless pit.

And he opened the bottomless pit; and there arose a smoke out of the pit, as the smoke of a great furnace; and the sun and the air were darkened by reason of the smoke of the pit.

And there came out of the smoke locusts upon the earth: and unto them was given power, as the scorpions of the earth have power." (Revelation 9:1–3)

The locust army mentioned are not locusts like some people depicted in pictures, but supernatural beings, whether fallen angels or demonic beings. They are soldiers all ready for battle. Their appearance is described below:

"And the shapes of the locusts were like unto horses prepared unto battle; and on their heads were as it were crowns like gold, and their faces were as the faces of men.

And they had hair as the hair of women, and their teeth were as the teeth of lions.

And they had breastplates, as it were breastplates of iron; and the sound of their wings was as the sound of chariots of many horses running to battle.

And they had tails like unto scorpions, and there were stings in their tails: and their power was to hurt men five months." (Revelation 9:7–10)

The prophet Joel also mentions this locust army in detail in chapter 2.

"Blow ye the trumpet in Zion, and sound an alarm in my holy mountain: let all the inhabitants of the land tremble: for the day of the LORD cometh, for it is nigh at hand;

A day of darkness and of gloominess, a day of clouds and of thick darkness, as the morning spread upon the mountains: a great people and a strong; there hath not been ever the like, neither shall be any more after it, even to the years of many generations.

A fire devoureth before them; and behind them a flame burneth: the land is as the garden of Eden before them, and behind them a desolate wilderness; yea, and nothing shall escape them.

The appearance of them is as the appearance of horses; and as horsemen, so shall they run.

Like the noise of chariots on the tops of mountains shall they leap, like the noise of a flame of fire that devoureth the stubble, as a strong people set in battle array.

Before their face the people shall be much pained: all faces shall gather blackness.

They shall run like mighty men; they shall climb the wall like men of war; and they shall march every one on his ways, and they shall not break their ranks:

Neither shall one thrust another; they shall walk every one in his path: and when they fall upon the sword, they shall not be wounded.

They shall run to and fro in the city; they shall run upon the wall, they shall climb up upon the houses; they shall enter in at the windows like a thief.

The earth shall quake before them; the heavens shall tremble:

the sun and the moon shall be dark, and the stars shall withdraw their shining:

And the LORD shall utter his voice before his army (saints): for his camp is very great: for he is strong that executeth his word: for the day of the LORD is great and very terrible; and who can abide it?" (Joel 2:1–11)

They could be fallen angels because Jude mentions that angels are under darkness unto the judgement of the great day:

"And the angels which kept not their first estate, but left their own habitation, he hath reserved in everlasting chains under darkness unto the judgment of the great day." (Jude 1:6)

The destroyer and the locust army will cause the Earth to quake, as well as the Earth to become a desolate wilderness:

"A fire devoureth before them; and behind them a flame burneth: the land is as the garden of Eden before them, and behind them a desolate wilderness; yea, and nothing shall escape them." (Joel 2:3)

"The earth shall quake before them; the heavens shall tremble: the sun and the moon shall be dark, and the stars shall withdraw their shining." (Joel 2:10)

When will the day of the Lord occur?

According to scripture, no one knows the day or the hour. However, when Jesus returns to the Earth, the day of the Lord arrives with him.

"But of that day and hour knoweth no man, no, not the angels of heaven, but my Father only. But as the days of Noewere, so shall also the coming of the Son of man be. For as in the days that were before the flood they were eating and drinking, marrying and giving in marriage, until the day that Noe entered into the ark, And knew not until the flood came, and took them all away; so shall also the coming of the Son of man be." (Matthew 24:36–39)

"And I beheld when he had opened the sixth seal, and, lo, there was a great earthquake; and the sun became black as sackcloth of hair, and the moon became as blood; And the stars of heaven fell unto the earth, even as a fig tree casteth her untimely figs, when she is shaken of a mighty wind. And the heaven departed as a scroll when it is rolled together; and every mountain and island were moved out of their places. And the kings of the earth, and the great men, and the rich men, and the chief captains, and the mighty men, and every bondman, and every free man, hid themselves in the dens and in the rocks of the mountains; And said to the mountains and rocks, Fall on us, and hide us from the face of him that sitteth on the throne, and from the wrath of the Lamb: For the great day of his wrath is come; and who shall be able to stand?" (Revelation 6:12–17)

I became inspired one day and wrote this poem about the day of the Lord. I thought I would share it with you:

> The earth will tremble at the presence of Almighty God.
> The stars will fall from the sky.
> Humble yourselves and repent!
> For the day of the Lord draws nigh.
> It's a day of darkness, of trumpet sounds!
> The sun will turn black.
> The moon will go blood red.
> All this has been all written and said
> by the prophets of old.
> All this has been foretold.
> It's a day of terror, torment, and fear.
> So repent, all sinners!
> For the day of the Lord draws near.

At the hospital, my brain was in severe pain. I felt the weight of my head and thought I was going to die at any moment. I complained to the nurse about my head, and she wanted to lower my bed down, but I yelled out, "Don't!" out of fear of death. My head was all scarred inside, and putting the bed down would have killed me, I thought. The doctors decided to do an CT scan immediately, but as I was about to take the test, the pain was supernaturally healed. The Lord had healed me. I felt his power run inside my head just before they took the scan. I became annoyed that I was healed because I thought I had something to prove to the doctors. I wanted the doctors to see just how bad I was and that I was telling the truth. The Lord, however, knew what he was doing, and from that point on, I had no scarring inside my head. I was completely healed by the Lord. Just before the test was about to commence, I fell asleep, as I believe they must have drugged me at this point. I was knocked out cold.

I had a glimpse of the hospital staff transferring me, as they placed me in an isolation room all by myself. This room was creepy and old, with a mattress on the floor. I was confused and dazed at the time of waking up from the drugs that knocked me out in the first place. I sat up and saw a nurse standing in the doorway. Her eyes were fixed on mine as she was holding up a newspaper, and it shocked me. I don't know why, but I thought Violet died because of how this woman presented herself. She just stood there. *Who was she?* I thought. *Was she working for Satan? Or was it something that the mental health nurses do?* It felt as if the nurse was taunting me with the newspaper. My memory suddenly lapsed over, and then the room shifted.

I thought I was in hell for real. An eternally lost feeling came upon me. It made me think I was lost for all eternity, not ever being allowed to leave. I was locked in an asylum, in the depths of hell itself, I thought. I was not dressed in my clothes but had a hospital gown on. I looked around this cell and felt completely lost. A spirit of a woman's face appeared on a plaque which was attached to the wall. It started to change faces. I jumped back away from the wall and freaked out. This spirit convinced me that this was my eternal punishment, being locked in a cell with a spirit to torment me. It sent a searing pain down through my body. I was so afraid and felt tormented. I stood up and began to yell and point at the spirit, trying to rebuke it.

I quickly got on my knees and prayed with all my heart to the Lord, asking him for a second chance and to let me leave this tormenting place. I was really scared by this experience, which had left me without hope. Being lost forever and ever is something I never want to experience again. I gave up praying and then realised that the door was open. I got up and went outside to find a bathroom. I arrived at the bathroom and heard a spirit ask me, "Would you marry Satan? He is Jesus' brother." I said yes without even realising what I just said. It occurred to me later that the demon also wanted me to sell my soul to Satan. I knew that Satan isn't Jesus' brother; this is a lie from the devil.

I saw a nurse, but she didn't speak to me. I walked away from her to discover another room, then walked outside and looked at the walls, unsure of where I was. I saw the light reflecting back off the walls and walked around without a clue. I was lost. My mind was gone.

I had been brought to a maximum security mental health facility. I followed the nurse as she silently directed me to this place. No one spoke to me the entire time, making this experience a living nightmare. I was taken in silence to a single bedroom, where I saw another patient who asked me if I was pregnant. I looked down at my stomach, and something made me think I was. A thought entered my mind from the devil: The closed rooms were sacrificing rooms in which to kill newborn babies. I panicked. I went to another bathroom, thinking I couldn't live in hell any longer, and attempted to drown myself. As I tried, the Lord took the water out from inside my body. I truly didn't want to kill myself but just wanted to leave hell. By killing myself, I would have ended up there.

I returned to my bedroom and kneeled down to pray, but I saw a demonic-looking dwarf in the mirror, staring at me with a weird-looking head and a nasty grin across its face. As I looked in the mirror, the demon just sat beside me; when I turned from the mirror to see the demon, it wasn't there, but it was there in the mirror. I just stared at the mirror until the demon left.

Joshua and the children came to visit me. When I saw them, I recognised them and forgot about the ordeal at the apartment building completely. I didn't see them as demons or Satan anymore, as this left my mind. I was just so happy to see them all and remembered just how much I loved my children.

My in-laws, Tina and Andrew, flew out and came to my family's aid when they heard about my situation. They assisted Joshua in looking after the children and encouraged my own family to visit me. Tina and Andrew visited me every day in hospital, and after three days, they decided to take the children back home with them, while Joshua remained by my side.

September 28, 2015, was the night of the super blood moon. I was looking forward to seeing it, because I missed the blood moons each time they appeared that year and in 2014; due to cloudy nights, I never got to see one. However, I thought I could catch a glimpse of this one while on my holiday, as the weather was forecasted for a clear night. I also heard a few Christians say that maybe the rapture would happen on this date. I started to believe that this was possible and kept an open mind about it.

That night, I went outside into the courtyard and suddenly heard the sounds of horsemen riding by. I believed that they were the horsemen of the Apocalypse. I know that they didn't actually ride by me; however, at the time, it appeared this way. I know now by reading scripture that the riders on the white, red, black, and pale horse are actually already riding throughout the Earth. They are not really the horsemen of the Apocalypse, like everyone thinks they are. They are actually here to kill with hunger, sword, beasts, and death.

"And I saw, and behold a white horse: and he that sat on him had a bow; and a crown was given unto him: and he went forth conquering, and to conquer. And when he had opened the second seal, I heard the second beast say, Come and see.

And there went out another horse that was red: and power was given to him that sat thereon to take peace from the earth, and that they should kill one another: and there was given unto him a great sword.

And when he had opened the third seal, I heard the third beast say, Come and see. And I beheld, and lo a black horse; and he that sat on him had a pair of balances in his hand.

And I heard a voice in the midst of the four beasts say, A measure of wheat for a penny, and three measures of barley for a penny; and see thou hurt not the oil and the wine.

And when he had opened the fourth seal, I heard the voice of the fourth beast say, Come and see.

And I looked, and behold a pale horse: and his name that sat on him was Death, and Hell followed with him. And power was given unto them over the fourth part of the earth, to kill with sword, and with hunger, and with death, and with the beasts of the earth." (Revelation 6:2–8)

If we look at Death, he is actually an enemy of God. This is the rider on the pale horse that is depicted in the book of Revelation. Death will be the last enemy to be destroyed and put into the lake of fire.

"The last enemy that shall be destroyed is death." (1 Corinthians 15:26)

"And death and hell were cast into the lake of fire. This is the second death." (Revelation 20:14)

Satan was the one who had the power of death:

"Forasmuch then as the children are partakers of flesh and blood, he also himself likewise took part of the same; that through death he might destroy him that had the power of death, that is, the devil." (Hebrews 2:14)

Jesus now has the keys of hell and death:

"I am he that liveth, and was dead; and, behold, I am alive for evermore, Amen; and have the keys of hell and of death." (Revelation 1:18)

The book of Job gives us some clues about the horsemen. I'll give you a few verses, and you decide if it fits:

"Destruction and death say, We have heard the fame thereof with our ears." (Job 28:22)

"In famine he shall redeem thee from death: and in war from

the power of the sword. Thou shalt be hid from the scourge of the tongue: neither shalt thou be afraid of destruction when it cometh. At destruction and famine thou shalt laugh: neither shalt thou be afraid of the beasts of the earth." (Job 5:20–22)

While in the courtyard, I wondered about looking at the stars. At this moment, the false Jesus came and said, "I'm going to rapture you" I fell for it again. I looked up at the moon and saw beams of light rising up towards the moon: another vision from the devil. I thought that the rapture had just happened, and I waited eagerly for it, but it was too late. It then occurred to me that I was left behind in the Great Tribulation. This is when I still believed in a pre-tribulation rapture.

During this time, three hospital workers approached me. They grabbed me and attempted to take me inside the facility. I panicked, thinking that the staff wanted to sacrifice me inside. It felt so real what Satan did; it really felt as if I was going to be sacrificed. As soon as the hospital workers touched me, I was hit hard again by demons. A whirlwind of terror and fear hit me. My reality shifted dramatically as I was dragged by the demons. Time and space seemed to speed up around me, as I was ripped by demons, mentally and physically. I was left broken and hurt by the hospital staff, for I tried to fight back hard against the demons and the staff. The hospital staff did not realise what had happened to me, and I was in too much pain to respond. They drugged me and left me on the grass, crying my eyes out. As I moved my foot with my eyes still shut, I felt dead body parts lying next to me. The flesh felt solid, and I knew it was a mass grave surrounding me. It was my worst nightmare coming true. (This is what Satan can really do to a person.) I lay there and cried out like a child. I said, "Jesus, I love you!" referring to my Lord and Saviour: not the demon but our Lord Jesus.

The next minute, I was placed into my bed by the staff. All battered and bruised by the experience, I started to physically recover supernaturally. It was our God healing me completely; he took away my physical pain. During the night, I heard dramatic voices in the air; I was told I was going to be crucified and killed on a cross. I continuously heard all these uneasy comments and sound effects until I finally crashed out.

The next day, the Lord helped me. I started to see demons around me, so I began singing "In the Name of Jesus." The name Jesus came to me in a vision. As I was singing this song, Jesus' name blocked out the demons that were appearing in front of my eyes.

When Joshua arrived at the hospital, he gave me the Bible that was in my handbag; I had asked him to bring it. I opened the Bible and turned to 1 Chronicles. As I was trying to read the first chapter, an evil spirit came to me. He stood next to me and began to pronounce some of the names to me. He wanted to show me that he could read the Bible well. I knew that it was an evil spirit and not me reading these words. I found it difficult to pronounce these names without someone reading them back to me. He was able to read each name to me without making an error. I stopped interacting with him and walked away from the spirit.

A few days later, I was moved to a less secure area of the mental health facility. I started to recover more once I saw my father and younger brother, Samuel, who travelled the distance to see me. I played soccer with Samuel, and it kind of brought me back. I told them Satan attacked me and tried to convince my family what took place in my life. Samuel didn't believe my story and looked at it as only psychosis.

Aunt Kelly gave me a Christian book during my stay in hospital. However, I didn't have the opportunity to read it myself, as I saw a lady who was depressed and missing her child, so I gave it to her to read. I witnessed to her about our Lord Jesus, and I prayed for her. She was grateful and took the book. She told me she was reading it, and I told her to keep it, knowing it could bring her to the Lord Jesus.

I decided to walk around and headed out to the courtyard. I saw another woman standing on a table in a very unusual yoga position. I just looked at her and wondered. I decided to approach her and said something. Surprisingly, she just hissed at me like a snake. I stepped back, realising she had a spirit inside of her. I saw another lady holding tarot cards and told her that she shouldn't read them. She hated me from that moment on and made others hate me. I was more relaxed at this new facility; I was extremely nice to the nurses and asked them if they wanted prayer.

The entire time I was there, I hadn't realised I was in hospital. I couldn't comprehend it because no one told me where I was. It wasn't pointed out to me, and I was too sick to ask any questions. I was finally discharged seven days later, driving back home with my father and Joshua.

CHAPTER 8

FINALLY HOME

WE FINALLY ARRIVED home from our nightmare holiday. The day we drove home happened to be our wedding anniversary; we celebrated nine years of marriage. The years had passed by so fast. I was relieved that we were still married because Satan and the demons had tried to separate us while on holidays. The situation that happened to me severely rocked our relationship.

The next morning, I constantly thought about the masquerade mask I had sitting in the glass cabinet. I wanted to grab a hammer and smash it to pieces. This mask had red feathers with a golden exterior and a golden bead in the middle of its forehead. As I came back to Christ, it felt wrong to have this mask. I knew I had to find a way to get rid of it. Although the mask cost $255, I wanted to destroy it; selling it was not an option.

That morning, while lying down next to Joshua, I asked him if I could get rid of the mask, as it was now haunting me. With a sense of defeat and hesitation, he looked at me and answered, "Yeah, fine."

As soon as he replied, I leapt out of bed, opened the glass cabinet, took out the mask, and ripped it into pieces. Joshua was surprised and upset at me for doing this. I wanted to get rid of any satanic thing I possessed, and this was the one thing that I really wanted to take out of my house.

Our children arrived home later that day, after staying with Tina and Andrew. I was racing around the house, trying to vacuum and tidy up, as I had the nurses coming over and wanted to clean up the house before they arrived. The nursing team were visiting to check up on me. I saw the children's many toys lying on the floor and started to pick them up. Joshua stopped me and said he would organise the toys and put them in their proper place (he wanted the toys arranged correctly). The nursing team arrived while I was vacuuming, which upset me because I didn't finish in time, and the toys were still lying in a great big mess, scattered all over the floor. Embarrassed by the state of the house, I gave up cleaning and started to communicate with the nurses. They stayed only a few minutes and left.

Straight after they left, Joshua and I got into an argument over the toys. I wanted to get rid of some, as there were too many, and just the idea of them got to me. I didn't want to see a single one on the floor. I completely lost the plot and called Sally to pick up myself and the children.

I told her, "I have had enough, and I am leaving Joshua for real."

My sister arrived at our house shortly after I phoned her. As I was packing to leave, a spirit started to speak to me.

He said, "Take the laptop with you to your sister's place so you will be able to complete your testimony."

However, this spirit wasn't from the Lord. I had just started to type my testimony out on the computer. I grabbed the laptop, stuffed it inside one of the bags I had packed for the children and myself, and drove off with Sally to her house. Tossing and unable to get any sleep at Sally's place, I got up and opened the laptop to continue typing up my testimony. The reason why I started to write my experience was to show my family and friends what Satan had done against me. I did not at all contemplate that it would turn into a book.

I tried hard to recall all my lost memories, which took place at home and during our holiday. Over time, these drastic memories returned after looking deeply back into my past. I could remember some of them, but some memories were blocked. I still couldn't recall them completely. After spending several hours on it, I somehow lost the file. It was gone: my whole testimony. I sat there grieved and so frustrated by it all.

The next day didn't get any better. "You are going to hell if you keep listening," a male voice said, which made me tremble. It really frightened me, thinking it was the Lord; however, this was a demon. In fear, I tried hard to stop speaking to the spirit that was lingering around me but failed.

My brother-in-law Jake and sister Sally invited their pastor and his wife to visit me. The pastor wanted to counsel me and began speaking. He started by offering me prayer and continued to ask if I am saved.

Frustrated by this question, I quickly replied, "Yes, I am."

They made me feel unsure if I truly was. Was I saved? Deep down inside, I was hurt by this question, knowing at the time I was trying hard to come back to God. I had spent every single day reading the Bible and playing hymns until I drove my husband mad. It wasn't until I discovered that YouTube channel that I lost my way from God, and as a result, I was seriously hurt by demons. I was unsure if I was saved now; I really just wanted to serve the Lord with all my heart and thought I was doing his will. I started to explain to them that I had been attacked by Satan, not understanding much about demons and their current involvement in my life at that time. This just left me feeling completely lost and alone.

I began to miss Joshua deeply. I decided to text him, to amend what I had done. I didn't want a divorce, and I wanted my marriage back. Joshua drove over to Sally's place to pick us up. We left Sally's house and drove off to Tina and Andrew's. An uneasy feeling of guilt sat inside my stomach. I shouldn't have taken off like I did. I ended up staying overnight with my in-laws, as Joshua didn't want me home alone with the children. I knew I made a mess of things with him. Unable to still have a good night sleep due to tormenting spirits, I got up the next morning feeling horrible. I had been running without proper sleep for days, but instead of being tired, I had the opposite problem.

That morning, the spirit again began to convince me by saying, "The nurses are coming over again to give you more medication." This was a lie from the demon. You see, I was agitated at the nurses for giving me a stronger dose of medication the night before. I didn't want them to return, as I felt like I lost my independence, which really annoyed me. I was being watched by the nurse while I took the medication. Not wanting to see the nurses again, I asked Joshua if I could go to Sally's house again before they came over. I really thought that the nurses were coming over again. He was tired after a long night at work and did not give me a full answer.

Wanting to leave the house, I said to my husband's family that I was going for a walk. Before I left the house, the spirit beckoned me to run. "Take your bag and run!" I heard the voice tell me. I should not have listened. I was upset at everyone at that stage. However, the spirit tricked me, and I listened to it once again.

I took off to the train station, running the entire way there. I decided to head to my grandmother's place. I wanted to prove to everyone that I was well enough to be alone. I just wanted my independence back. I really upset my husband and his family by running off.

I contacted Sally and spoke to her for a few minutes while waiting for the train to arrive. I told her that I was heading over to our grandmother's place and hung up. My uncle James picked me up from the station once I alighted from the train. I could have walked to my grandmother's house, but Sally had asked Uncle James to pick me up instead. I was surprised to see him standing at the exit gates of the station, waiting for me. I got into my uncle's car, and we drove to my grandmother's house. When we arrived, I felt guilty and became grieved for leaving my husband. I wanted to call him, but my father suddenly turned up at my grandmother's front door. Someone must have told him I was there.

He asked me, "Why didn't you attend church this morning?"

I was not aware that I was to attend his church that morning; I must have agreed with him on the way back from our trip. I didn't even know it was Sunday; I had spent all weekend running away from Joshua.

My cousin's wife Sarah was over also. I asked her if she wanted to go to the shops with me. My father drove us to the shopping centre. We were in a store when I cried out in pain, "I need an ambulance!"

It was supernatural; it hit me hard, and I couldn't move from it. I had chest pain. "What's going on?" I asked, panicked. I tried to reassure myself that this wasn't happening, as I couldn't bear the pain. My father and Sarah took me to the medical centre, where a doctor examined me and cleared me.

I recovered from the attack and felt fine, so we drove back to my grandmother's place. As soon as I arrived at my grandmother's front door, the supernatural chest pain returned. I knew that this feeling which came upon me was not a natural occurrence. Someone was causing me this pain.

"Take me to the hospital!" I cried out.

This time they listened, and I was rushed into the emergency ward, where I was admitted immediately.

I was waiting on the hospital bed; the nurse arrived and handed me some medication for the pain. Sally also turned up at the hospital, joining my father and Sarah.

Thoughts of Joshua again started running through my mind. I wondered what I had done. I left him again. I called him, but Sarah took the phone and began speaking to Joshua instead. I wanted him to know I wanted him back. I made a big mistake by taking off the way I did.

As I sat on the bed, my perception of reality shifted again. I saw Sarah's blue eyes staring back at me and began to see her as a demon. Torment surrounded me, and I felt trapped inside the hospital. However, I quickly took my King James Bible out of my handbag; I found Psalms 23, and Sarah started to read it:

"The LORD is my shepherd; I shall not want.

He maketh me to lie down in green pastures: he leadeth me beside the still waters.

He restoreth my soul: he leadeth me in the paths of righteousness for his name's sake.

Yea, though I walk through the valley of the shadow of death, I will fear no evil: for thou art with me; thy rod and thy staff they comfort me.

Thou preparest a table before me in the presence of mine enemies: thou anointest my head with oil; my cup runneth over.

Surely goodness and mercy shall follow me all the days of my life: and I will dwell in the house of the LORD forever."

During the reality shift, I felt the grip of death run through my body. I thought I was dying. After Sarah read the passage, I noticed the room turning back to normal and the torment leaving me. The grip of death also left me.

Shortly after things had returned to normal, the demon provoked me and said, "Witness for the Lord!" Pondering what I had just heard, I received some encouragement to approach a patient and witnessed to him about Jesus. I realised I did not know how to witness well but did my best with the knowledge I had. As I walked back to the bed, I spotted a male nurse, approached him, and spoke to him about Jesus. He looked at me as if something was wrong with me.

Sarah received a doctor's letter from the nursing staff, and she told me that they wanted me to be transferred to hospital closer to my house. I was still thinking it was for the chest pain. My father, Sally, Sarah, and I left the hospital and headed to my grandmother's place first.

We stopped over at my grandmother's place to grab a few sandwiches; the spirit told me, "Don't go to the hospital." I told my family that I was not going to the hospital and that I felt fine and just wanted to go to sleep.

"No, you have to go," Sarah said. I took her advice, and my father, Sally, Sarah, and a family friend drove me to the hospital.

We arrived at the hospital and walked up to the main entry. Sarah showed the nurse my letter, and she directed us to this secure facility outside the main hospital building. It was a mental health facility. At the time, I thought I was going back to hospital for my chest pain, but the doctors had other plans for me. I never did read what was written in that doctor's letter. However, one day I glanced at the computer screen at my local doctor, to find a letter which stated that I had delusions of God.

I was admitted again, thinking I was in the main hospital. Nobody told me that I had just been admitted into a mental health facility. The nurse directed me to my bed sometime after midnight, so I went to bed and settled in, but I was unable to sleep. "Get up and repent," a demon encouraged me. I began to cry my eyes out as I walked outside my ward. I knelt down on the ground and felt so much regret as my tears flowed down my face.

"You need to stop this," a male nurse warned me. I refused and began to cry harder, unable to hold it all back. Kneeling on the ground, with my eyes closed in fear, I was dragged away by two male nurses; they took me down the corridor and into another facility. This is when things became a little unusual; I do not recall anything after this moment.

I awoke in shock as I found myself in an isolation room: four walls, a glass window, and a solid metal door. The room was creepy and old, and the mattress was on the floor. As I approached the door to the outside of this room, I realised it was not locked. The door swung open, and I saw this bright blue room staring back at me. My whole world was shaken up. I walked outside into the blue room and wondered where I was.

I pondered in absolute shock as I walked around, looking at the faces of strangers. It took me a little while to realise that I was in a mental health facility. Why couldn't someone just speak to me directly and explain that I was going to a mental health facility? I began to get extremely angry. This set me off, and I no longer acted like a civil human being. I demanded to know my rights and asked to be discharged from this place, but they refused and held me against my will for seven weeks.

The nurse took me to my room and showed me my bed. As I sat on my bed, I pondered how to get out of this place. I contacted my family and yelled at everyone for leaving me behind at this facility. Angry and hurt by my family, I started to feel this urge around my mouth. I was able to talk in third person. A spirit entered me, convincing me that he was God, so I began to allow this spirit to speak through me.

I was trying to convince my entire family that God was speaking through me. The spirit which spoke through me told everyone that they were going to hell. Without understanding the demons, I just believed that I was allowing God our Father to speak through me. This is how a lot of people receive false prophecies by spirits speaking through them. Most are very subtle, and you cannot even tell that it is not from the Lord.

Joshua came to visit me. I allowed the spirit to warn him that he was going to die in a car accident. Dismissing these words, he thought I was just talking in third person. He was unable to distinguish the evil spirit that was speaking through my mouth. My family continued telling me this wasn't from the Lord, but I chose to be deceived willingly by an evil spirit. I didn't know the enemy could do such a thing. If someone just pointed out that I had a demon speaking through me, I might have woken up and realised this fact. However, no one did.

False prophecies: a phrase I want to remove from my life. I wrote several letters in the name of the Lord to my family members and friends, and delivered one to my grandmother's church on one of my day leaves from the mental health facility. The spirit portraying itself as Jesus came to me again. He directed what he wanted me to write down on paper. I was fasting one day when he came; he told me to write some prophecies down as he spoke. Scared I would be caught by the nursing staff, I hid myself away, taking some paper to write these prophecies on. I secretly recorded this spirit's message on this paper.

While in the facility, an old friend named Lisa came to visit. Lisa had just recently come back to Jesus. Sometime after she came back to Jesus, Lisa claimed that a demon had entered her. She went to visit her doctor and told him about the demon. The doctor instantly diagnosed her with schizophrenia. Lisa claimed she was no longer the same person and found it hard to work and to do the things she used to do easily because she became physically sick. Just to be clear: Christians can have demons.

I took on a bold personality whilst in the facility. My personality had changed completely; I was no longer the nice quiet girl who sat in hiding, shaking with fear from public speaking. My nerves had disappeared, and I didn't shake in fear any longer. God had changed me. I stood up one day while in the facility and read a chapter out loud to everyone from the Bible, reading Matthew 24. I felt the true Lord God helping me speak these words to everyone. As I began to read, a fight broke out between a few men, who started throwing chairs around. During this uproar, the true Lord God showed me that evil spirits were intervening, trying to stop these people from hearing the gospel.

A powerful demon came to me during my stay at the facility. It was the same booming voice from the hospital who was claiming to be God. This time, it was going to try and destroy me that much further. This demon started causing me physical pain by putting me on fire with an invisible flame. I felt the fire burning my body, which left me in agony. "Sing 'Amazing Grace,'" the demon said. I began to sing this in fear, trying hard to control the pain. I thought I was doomed. I sat on the couch and just took the pain. I was full of fear and couldn't recognise that it wasn't God doing this to me. I thought I was heading to hell. I was a confused mess at the time.

"Deny me," the same evil spirit spoke out, but I didn't want to deny the Lord. My heart suddenly became supernaturally faint and heavy. This feeling fell over me; it felt as if I was slipping from the Lord and unable to stand as a Christian. I suddenly said, "I'll deny you!" I was shocked at myself, as I had never spoken out against the Lord in my entire life.

He asked me, "Would you serve me, even if you are going to hell?"

"Yes, I would," I replied.

I thought I was done and that I was really going to hell. He gave me thirty years to live, and then he said I would go to hell. I fell deep into depression and was diagnosed with stage one psychosis (schizophrenia) by the doctors at the mental health facilities.

The supernatural chest pain returned. I knocked on the door to the nursing station, and the nurse opened. I tried informing the nurse about my pain and explained that I needed to go to the main building of the hospital for treatment, but all they could do was give me medication. I felt like Satan just wanted to kill me. I was in agony, as I sat in a chair almost dying and unable to receive more medical assistance. I was desperate; no one took me seriously, and no one came to my aid. I ended up lying on the ground in agony until the pain disappeared.

The booming male demon attacked me again, this time hitting me hard across my head by simply yelling at me. My brain felt supernaturally sunk inside my skull, and this insane feeling of death attached itself to me. I strolled around the facility, thinking, *This is it ... I'm going to pass away.* I just could not recover. As I arrived to my room, I crashed on the hospital bed and fell asleep instantly.

The next day, I awoke and realised that I was still alive. I had not passed away. I did not think I would see another day. I started to become very sick physically from being tormented by the demons, and being locked up against my will didn't help me. My mind started to crumble and wither away. I started to feel like my body was going to die from imprisonment. My spirit had begun to want to let go.

The torment kept on coming, though. One day, I was in so

much torment that I ended up falling to the ground in front of my family. Nearly every time I saw my family, my eyes would become shut supernaturally. I could feel the effects of the supernatural touch on my eyes, and my speech became sluggish. I couldn't physically open my eyes or speak well. My entire family thought I had lost my mind. Satan just wanted to kill me, but instead he ruined my reputation.

I was controlled by the demons at this stage. I would listen to their every word. One day, as I was listening to a demon, I all of a sudden heard these words reach me: "Stop listening," it yelled in absolute power. It was an angelic being, and I knew it was from the Lord. An angel had just spoken to me. I immediately stopped what I was doing and asked myself, "Why am I listening?"

The instant that I asked this, something automatically clicked inside my brain. Immediately, my eyes were opened, and I realised that I was talking to demonic spirits and not God or Jesus. I stopped listening to the demons instantly and realised I was deceived by Satan.

Knowing full well now I was speaking to demons, I decided to ask the spirit, who was portraying itself as our Lord Jesus, whether he was from the Lord, like it states in 1 John 4:1–3:

"Beloved, do not believe every spirit, but test the spirits, whether they are of God; because many false prophets have gone out into the world. Hereby know ye the Spirit of God: Every spirit that confesseth that Jesus Christ is come in the flesh is of God: And every spirit that confesseth not that Jesus Christ is come in the flesh is not of God: and this is that spirit of antichrist, whereof ye have heard that it should come; and even now already is it in the world."

"No, I'm from the enemy," the spirit replied.

It stayed with me a little while longer and then suddenly left. I haven't heard from it since. The spirit which was portraying itself as God stopped tormenting me, and I was finally awake and no longer asleep.

After seven long weeks, I was finally discharged from the mental health facility after a successful court hearing. In this time period, Joshua and I reconciled our marriage and remained together. I also forgave my family for leaving me in the facility. This place really distressed me a lot. I know nurses are trained to help; I was once a nurse and know how hard this job can be. The only thing I want to say to mental health nurses is please tell these patients what going on with their situation. Don't leave them in the dark, like I was. Not one person told me that I had psychosis or schizophrenia. Not the doctor or the nurses. I had to find out by looking at a piece of paper that my case manager brought out. It really upset me because I really didn't understand why I was locked up and why I was held against my own will for seven weeks. Also, no one could comprehend that I was going through a spiritual battle. Everyone thought I was just mentally sick. Mental health is just one major area that Satan likes to attack people. I had just experienced what it truly felt like.

"For we wrestle not against flesh and blood, but against principalities, against powers, against the rulers of the darkness of this world, against spiritual wickedness in high places." (Ephesians 6:12)

CHAPTER 9

NIGHTMARES

I ARRIVED HOME AT last and began to recover from the mental anguish of being locked up. I was extremely ill at this stage and could feel a sense of physical sickness through my entire body. I couldn't do anything, but I quickly realised that I hardly had any help and no choice. I pushed myself to my breaking point. I also knew that if I could not cope and look after my children well enough, I could lose custody of them. I wanted to keep my family together, but Satan and the demons continued to make life extremely hard for me.

When I left the hospital, my nightmares became worse; however, with the Lord's help, my mind also became sound. I was not deluded by the demons anymore, and my perception of reality had stopped shifting. Satan could not alter my reality any longer, and even if he did try, I would now recognise it. God was truly back in my life and helping me. I also returned to God completely and stopped watching Anne's YouTube videos.

The demons began to tempt me through severe sexual temptations. This would come over me by the demons internally dwelling inside my body as well as the demons that entered my house. It felt different this time, as it was not the same attack as before, when the demons entered my body and tried to give me an orgasm. This time, they wanted me to willingly seek and desire this feeling. It was an extremely lustful desire that they placed over me; I could hardly say no to this. However, I said no and refused this temptation also. As they tempted me, they would say, "I just want you to lose some weight, sexualise yourself, and have sex with all the demons." After this, a severe sexual desire ran through the lower parts of my body. The demons were trying to lure me away from God and accept this sexual desire they offered me.

As I was falling asleep one night, I suddenly felt a spirit lifting up my hand and feet as well as triggering me to wake me up. I also heard a loud bang in the ceiling to grab my attention. This was the beginning of the spiritual warfare that I was facing every day. My life had just changed severely. I was given a lot of faith and knew I would never be the same.

I started to notice that demons were interacting within my dreams. They would take me to scenes and talk to me while in this dreaming state. The demons used my dreams to communicate with me and torment me most nights. I want to give you a few examples of these types of dreams.

I dreamt that I was in this dark place. It was a creepy night, and I saw the planets in our solar system drift by, with military planes following them. Then in another scene, I heard Satan's voice. He said, "You want to challenge me?" He said this because when I turned to Jesus after I repented, I stupidly proclaimed out of the blue, not thinking, "I want to challenge Satan." This was before the devils attacked me. I awoke, grieved, and put the bed sheet over my head. I truly believe Satan drew me to say these words. I felt unusual the day I said it.

On another night, I dreamt that I was chasing a white spirit and caught it. After I caught this spirit, my head suddenly began to hurt immensely. I thought I was going to die within this dream. In this dreaming state, I called out, "Jesus, I love you," out of fear and shock. My mind returned back to normal instantly; my two-year-old started to cry, waking me out of my dream. As I switched the light on, I had a vision of our Lord Jesus, with a beautiful light surrounding him, and he said, "You will be saved." I knew instantly that it was him. His presence alone told me.

I carried my child back to my room, and we fell asleep. She woke up and vomited on my bed sheets. I became upset, as it was early morning, and I could hardly move. I washed the bed sheets and hung them on the clothes line out back. I was wondering if the sheets would be okay, pondering that it might rain overnight. My mind was full of worries, being unable to organise myself; everything weighed heavily on my mind.

My daughter and I shared my bed that morning. As I went to sleep, a dream came to me, which went something along these lines: As I was hanging bed linens on the clothes line, I saw black, heavy clouds in the air. I took off the bed linen and decided to hang them up inside the spare room. I went looking for the pegs, which led me to the kitchen and dining room. I could see the moon and the black night sky, but inside my house, I could see daylight. I had a glimpse of a baby in a UFO ship flying through the night sky, and then the most horrifically insane feeling began to grip me. I became aware that I was in a dream and tried really hard to call upon Jesus for help. I managed to speak the words "Jesus, we have the victory," within this dream. As I spoke these words, a few demons screeched in fear, and the insane feeling disappeared.

Within another dream, I dreamt I was standing on the top of a waterfall. I saw someone watching a child playing at the edge of this waterfall, when all of a sudden, the conditions changed, and the people all disappeared. I suddenly hung on for dear life, holding onto a part of the waterfall within a cave. I held on with one hand; the other hand was holding onto my husband's expensive camera. As I hung there, the water was flowing rapidly down my body. I also looked like Blade from my daydream world. She was once again present within a dream. "Let go of the camera," a demon said to me. I refused to let go of it, as I did not want to lose it. The demon continued, "It's wet anyway," so I began to pray, and I said in faith,

"Jesus! Please keep me in the cave." I heard a voice say "Satan." Then the scene changed, and I fell into a car. A torch light was directed at my face, instantly waking me out of this dream.

What I am about to share with you was not a dream; it happened to me while I was wide awake. I was lying on my bed one night, and my eyes suddenly became open to the daydreaming world. It was like a vision. I saw a hand appear in front of me, and it beckoned me to follow it toward an open door. Curiosity entered my mind, but I decided not to follow the hand. After I said no to the devil, the hand and door disappeared from my vision. The devil attempted to entice me to see what was behind the door. I was intrigued by it and wondered what the devil would have shown me had I have taken the bait.

Early one morning, I heard a voice tell me, "I will deliver you." I felt a presence enter the room. I was asleep, but I was also wide awake at the same time. This was not a dream because I was well aware that I had heard these words loud and clear, in a gentle male voice. There was a pause in which I was given an opportunity to reply to him. "Thank you," was all I could say in return. I had a happy smile across my face, as I knew it was God.

I had been praying to the Lord for over a year, asking him which church was the right one for me to attend. I eagerly wanted to know where I could go that held the truth. One evening, I was praying to the Lord, and he suddenly spoke through me. He directed me not to go to my father's church; instead, I was told to attend the Slavic Assembly of God church. This was the church my grandmother attends. I just knew it was God who spoke these words through me. I know it sounds like when I was deceived by the evil spirits, but this time, I didn't confuse this voice for an evil spirit, so without hesitation, I left the Message Believing church. I believe the reason why I was told to no longer attend my father's church was because it contains the messages taught by William Branham.

The church my family used to attend closed down, my father found a Message Believers church about twenty minutes away from where I lived. He started to fellowship with this congregation. I decided to attend this church after I repented, knowing full well I did not really believe the message of William Branham in the first place. I attended this church because of the short distance from our house, and I enjoyed being amongst these people. However, I did spend some time looking at his message and found that they did not fit the Bible well.

I listened to the Lord and left the Message Believers church. I started to attend the Slavic Assembly of God church, as directed by the Lord. I went on a Saturday evening and arrived there just before six o'clock. I said hello to the pastor, feeling extremely awkward because I handed a false prophecy to this church while I was in the mental health facility. I had met the pastor a few times before this visit. For some strange reason, while I was locked up in the mental health facility, I asked him to come and visit me and to pray over me while I was under spiritual attack. However, I did not know him well.

I walked to an empty seat and sat down. The pastor rose and commenced the service. As the musicians began to play a song in the Slavic language, I started to follow the lyrics but found it difficult to sing correctly. As I tried my hardest to sing in that language, I felt God's presence as he corrected my tongue to be able to sing the song. I could barely read the Slavic language, so I knew this was the Lord's doing. He was showing me that the Lord was among his people. I could not believe what I had just witnessed, so I immediately stopped myself from singing, pondering in surprise what I had just experienced.

On another day, I told Grandmother May about this supernatural experience with the Lord. She was not surprised by it; however, what upset me was that she did not believe the Lord had sent me to her church. She believed that this Assembly of God church taught that there are three Gods, and she was taught to believe in only one, referring to Jesus-only doctrines and Trinitarian beliefs on the Godhead. I heard all of this growing up. She still believed that I was slightly deluded and deceived by Satan, like I was in the mental health facility.

"The Lord did direct me there," I told her. "This is the truth."

I was upset and unable to get it through to her what the Bible really teaches about our Father in heaven, Jesus, and the Holy Spirit. You cannot change a person's mind once it is made up. No matter how hard you try to tell them the truth, only God can change a person, unless they are open-minded towards the truth. Otherwise, they are not willing to change. Most people think what they believe in is really the truth.

I told Grandmother May, "Yes, there is only one God but three who bear record in heaven." At this moment, the Lord Jesus spoke through me and tried to correct her. His presence told me he was upset at her for going against him.

My father found out that I left the Message Believing church. I explained to him that I was directed by the Lord to leave this church during prayer.

He became frustrated at me and told me, "It's not from the Lord."

I tried hard to explain to him that it was, and this was the reason why I left this church. This church had asked me to return to them, but I could not. I had nothing against them; they truly look and act as decent Christians, but it was about the Lord, and he told me to leave them.

Another time, I spoke to my father on the phone, trying to convince him that William Branham's doctrines on the Godhead were incorrect. Branham believed that the Godhead contained one God with three offices or titles: Father, Son, and Holy Spirit. This is incorrect. As I was trying to convince my father, Jesus suddenly spoke through me again. He spoke to my father regarding this subject. I cannot remember what the Lord exactly said to my father. I was more intrigued at the fact that he chose to speak directly through me again. I knew it was the Lord Jesus, as his presence once again told me it was him. I should have paid a bit more attention to his words. However, I knew Jesus was going against this idea of the Godhead that William Branham taught.

I was at my new church one Sunday morning for the ten o'clock service when a little old Slavic woman who had never spoken to me before approached me and said, "The Lord gave me a vision of you, and I went and prayed for you straight away."

I was surprised by this. Her husband told me that he took up a five-day fast for me. I was grateful to the Lord for their willingness to help me, but I just could not understand how he could fast for me. He did not even know me.

One day, I was standing at the bathroom sink when I received these words from the song "Jesus Loves Me": The lyrics were "He will wash away my sins and let his little child come in." I cried because it touched me. Before God gave me these experiences, I was scared. Was I saved? I felt unworthy to enter into his kingdom, and it gave me great hope that I was not perishing.

Another day, the Lord Jesus spoke through me again and said, "You have sickness." At the time, I did not know that I was truly sick, but I thought it was all to do with demonic attacks. I know that unclean spirits can cause sickness in the body, and a good example is this verse from Luke 13:11–13:

"And, behold, there was a woman which had a spirit of infirmity eighteen years, and was bowed together, and could in no wise lift up herself. And when Jesus saw her, he called her to him, and said unto her, Woman, thou art loosed from thine infirmity. And he laid his hands on her: and immediately she was made straight, and glorified God."

During all of this, I have felt demonic sickness from demons, but I believe not every sickness comes from a demon.

CHAPTER 10

RUINED

One morning, amnesia set in when I awoke from my sleep. I had lost my mind. Fear fell over me, and in this confused state, I somehow called out, "Jesus!" I do not know how I called out to him, as I could not even remember the Lord. However, his name came out of my mouth. As soon as I called out to him, my mind was quickly restored, and I could recall who I was once again. I had completely forgotten everything. This was a scary experience; I could never imagine losing myself again.

One day, I was in the bathroom when a few demons started speaking to me. Suddenly, an angel spoke out loud to the demons and said, "You have ruined her life."

Knowing it was an angel that spoke, I wondered how the demons had ruined my life. I was not thinking clearly when I pondered this thought. In the past, I was planning to have another child, but when I was locked up in the mental health facility, a demon came to me and suggested not to have another child. I was so ill from the sickness that I actually agreed with the demon. Joshua and I also decided that I should not have another child due to my illness. It saddened me a lot because the spirit put this thought inside my head first.

I was brushing my teeth while facing the bathroom mirror, when all of a sudden, my body became possessed for a few seconds.

My face turned scary as I viewed myself. I never thought I could be possessed in this way. However, it never happened again. I was possessed, and I was a Christian. This happened so fast that I did not even have time to call upon Jesus for help. I really believe Christians underestimate what demons are truly capable of doing to them.

As a teenager, I heard a thought enter my mind one horrible night, and it said, "Blaspheme the Holy Spirit."

This was one of the first times I was attacked in this manner. I was in torment over this attack, thinking it was my own mind which was thinking up such things. I never thought about demons at the time, but they were the ones introducing this idea. I immediately turned to the Bible; I looked up scripture and repeated the words, "No, never, never," referring to the blasphemies coming from inside my mind. The scriptures also state that if you blaspheme the Holy Spirit, you will not be forgiven in this life as well as in the next life. This was why I was extremely afraid when these thoughts entered my mind. I cried to God during this attack, and these demons left.

One day in my mid-twenties, these thoughts returned, but this time, I was deep in sin and did not turn to the Lord. Instead, I pumped up the secular music to drown out these thoughts. I also quickly entered into the daydream world to get away from these words. I just wanted to completely forget. I was so afraid to blaspheme the Holy Spirit.

The other day, I was sitting at home when I heard a similar voice saying, "Blaspheme the Holy Spirit." It was overwhelming, and it hit me hard; the fear from my teenage years had returned to haunt me. I had to resist with all my heart not to be brainwashed into cursing God.

The unclean spirit repeatedly said after the attack, "You have blasphemed against the Holy Spirit; you are going to hell."

It was tormenting me, and it really felt like it was coming from inside my mind with such thoughts, but it was not my voice. It was a male's voice from a demon, and it was not attached to my own thoughts. I wasn't the one thinking up these words. This is how I could tell it was not coming directly from my own mind.

I visited Grandmother May's house, and we decided to sing a few songs to the Lord. However, my heart was not into singing to the Lord, and I started to become annoyed by it all. I had also been upset by all the attacks I had received. While I was there, I received this song from the Lord, which is translated from the Slavic language: "God, you are love because you save me."

One day, I decided to confront Anne about her channel. I sat down and wrote a message of warning to her. I then saw her transcript of one of her messages and read a small amount. I realised just how far from the truth this woman was. I still do not understand why I ever went onto her channel in the first place. However, reading the Bible again made all false doctrines leave my mind, and I began to conduct an in-depth study on the subjects of unclean spirits and Satan. I wanted to know the truth from scripture directly on these subjects and understand who I was actually dealing with.

I started searching places to see where I could be delivered. I searched websites for an answer and found a Christian healing service. I was hoping to seek deliverance from the Lord by attending this place. While I was in the bathroom, I was singing a song named "Tis So Sweet to Trust in Jesus." When I reached the part where I was to say "trust," I became possessed and said, "Lust." It got me angry. Could a Christian become possessed? Most Christians believe they cannot.

As I went to sleep, I dreamt that I saw an old lady turn into a gross-looking demon right in front of my eyes. While I was viewing this image of her, the most frightening fear hit me. I was trying to get the words out of my mouth to rebuke the demon but could not remember anything but absolute fear. I just could not get a word out until after the attack happened. I woke up and went into the shower. I was getting ready to head off to work when I heard an audible tune reach me. It was an old song that I had not heard since my childhood, called "Something Beautiful":

"He made something beautiful,
Something good all my confusion he understood,
All I had to offer him was brokenness and strife,
But he made something beautiful out of my life."

It was amazing that God could give me a song that I had completely forgotten. This was a song I used to sing, and it reminded me of my childhood.

One day, I said, "I wonder what my daydreaming could have been like if I was for Satan." I forgot that we are held accountable to the Lord for every idle word spoken. I went to pray when I was suddenly directed in my prayer again not to listen to the demons and not to go against God. I became concerned and asked God for forgiveness. God corrected me. I started to cry and was scared by my choice of words. It is a hard thing to take when you are corrected by the Lord.

In a dream, I saw a row of metal seats. I chose to sit down, and in my hand was my iPod. I automatically had this strong desire to play it and re-enter my daydream world. When this desire entered me, I suddenly started to hear a Christian song come through to me while deep within this dream. Being wide awake in my dream, I decided to toss my iPod away into the lake, which was in front of me. I woke up out of the dream and received these two songs from the Lord: "They Shall Be Showers of Blessing" and 'My Life Is in You, Lord."

I was feeling down for several days with the feeling that I was going to give up and collapse. If it was not for my children, I would have collapsed already. I am in such a bad state right now, and I have been fighting with myself not to collapse or give up. I am constantly calling out to the Lord day and night with tears, asking him for help.

One night, I was lying down on the bed next to Joshua when I was hit hard by a spirit, which swooped down and knocked me to the side of the bed. I was not hurt, but my body shifted. When will all these attacks stop?

CHAPTER 11

LUCIFER AND SATAN

PLEASE DON'T JUDGE me until you read through this chapter. I decided one day to consider who Lucifer was; was he really the same being as Satan? I was reading the book of Job and read how the sons of God, which are angels of God, presented themselves before the Lord, and Satan came among them. *Satan came among them?* I thought. Something suddenly clicked inside my brain, and for the very first time, it made sense: Satan is evil! Nowhere in the Bible had it ever mentioned that Lucifer and Satan were the same being. The Lord Jesus always addressed the devil as Satan. He never addressed him as Lucifer at all. Look and read for yourselves to see if you can really connect the two together as one being:

"But some of them said, He [Jesus] casteth out devils through Beelzebub the chief of the devils. And others, tempting him, sought of him a sign from heaven. But he, knowing their thoughts, said unto them, Every kingdom divided against itself is brought to desolation; and a house divided against a house falleth. If Satan also be divided against himself, how shall his kingdom stand?" (Luke 11:15–18)

I knew instantly that Satan and Lucifer were two separate beings, but as this thought entered my mind, I suddenly had a demon hit me hard against my body. It became extremely angry with me as it repeated what I had just thought about Satan, and then it immediately disappeared. I knew the demon could read my thoughts and gestures. Some Christians believe they cannot, but I am telling you out of my own personal experience that they can.

After the demon attacked me, I thought, *Did I just come across something?* I decided to continue looking into this subject. Most Christians know the story about how Lucifer became Satan. It goes something along these lines: Lucifer was one of God's angels. He rebelled against God by wanting to be like God. He took one-third of the angels into his service. He and the fallen angels were cursed by God and turned into Satan and the demons. The truth is angels are angels, and demons are demons. If all the angels who rebelled against God turned into demons, then why does it state in Jude 1:6 that the angels who left their own estate are in everlasting chains under darkness? Wouldn't they be demons, if this account of angels becoming demons was true? Also, as I was writing this, the Lord confirmed to me that angels are not demons. They are darkness, and so is Satan.

"And the angels which kept not their first estate, but left their own habitation, he hath reserved in everlasting chains under darkness unto the judgment of the great day." (Jude 1:6)

I'll give you another verse where this is not possible that these angels turned into demons. Not to also mention that this is not even recorded in the Bible.

Abaddon/Apollyon, who is the angel of the bottomless pit, is locked up in the pit. Wouldn't he also have become a demon?

"And they had a king over them, which is the angel of the bottomless pit, whose name in the Hebrew tongue is Abaddon, but in the Greek tongue hath his name Apollyon." (Revelation 9:11)

This is the verse I would like to show you:

"He cast upon them the fierceness of his anger, wrath, and indignation, and trouble, by sending evil angels among them." (Psalm 78:49)

God sent evil angels among the Egyptians before the Exodus of

Israel occurred. Evil angels, not devils, were sent to the Egyptians. Yes, some angels are evil and belong to Satan.

Please take a look at these verses:

"And there was war in heaven: Michael and his angels fought against the dragon [Satan]; and the dragon [Satan] fought and his angels." (Revelation 12:7)

"Then shall he say also unto them on the left hand, Depart from me, ye cursed, into everlasting fire, prepared for the devil and his angels." (Matthew 25:41)

I began to contemplate these questions about Lucifer and Satan, so I went straight to the Bible. Satan is the devil, the ancient serpent. So how then is his name Lucifer, who was a covering cherubim, a former angel of light? I also thought this. If the old serpent is the devil, wasn't he always the old serpent, a dragon? If he was an angel to begin with, why then does Satan transform into an angel of light? Angel transforming into an angel; it really does not make sense, right?

"And no marvel; for Satan himself is transformed into an angel of light." (1 Corinthians 11:14)

Where in the Bible is it written that Lucifer was cursed and turned into Satan? Where is it written that fallen angels were cursed and turned into what we now know as demons? Satan and his angels are cursed, but Satan is not Lucifer, and fallen angels are not demons.

"And I saw an angel come down from heaven, having the key of the bottomless pit and a great chain in his hand. And he laid hold on the dragon, that old serpent, which is the Devil, and Satan, and bound him a thousand years, And cast him into the bottomless pit, and shut him up, and set a seal upon him, that he should deceive the nations no more, till the thousand years should be fulfilled: and after that he must be loosed a little season." (Revelation 20:1–3)

According to scripture, God formed the light and created the darkness.

"I form the light, and create darkness: I make peace and create evil: I the Lord do all these things." (Isaiah 45:7)

Think about it: If Lucifer became Satan, then where does evil and darkness come from? God states that he created evil and darkness.

Satan is called the wicked one and the evil one.

"When anyone hears the word of the kingdom and does not understand it, the evil one comes and snatches away what has been sown in his heart." (Matthew 13:19)

Satan has a kingdom/domain:

"To open their eyes so that they may turn from darkness to light and from the dominion of Satan to God." (Acts 26:18)

Satan is an enemy of God:

"Another parable he put forth to them, saying: The kingdom of heaven is like a man who sowed good seed in his field; but while men slept, his enemy came and sowed tares among the wheat and went his way. But when the grain had sprouted and produced a crop, then the tares also appeared. So the servants of the owner came and said to him, 'Sir, did you not sow good seed in your field? How then does it have tares?' He said to them, 'An enemy has done this.' The servants said to him, 'Do you want us then to go and gather them up?' But he said, 'No, lest while you gather up the tares you also uproot the wheat with them. Let both grow together until the harvest, and at the time of harvest I will say to the reapers, "First gather together the tares and bind them in bundles to burn them, but gather the wheat into my barn."'" (Matthew 13:24–30)

"Then Jesus sent the multitude away and went into the house. And His disciples came to Him, saying, 'Explain to us the parable of the tares of the field.' He answered and said to them: 'He who sows the good seed is the Son of Man. The field is the world, the good seeds are the sons of the kingdom, but the tares are the sons of the wicked one. The enemy who sowed them is the devil, the harvest is the end of the age, and the reapers are the angels. Therefore as the tares are gathered and burned in the fire, so it will be at the end of this age. The Son of Man will send out His angels, and they will gather out of His kingdom all things that offend, and those who practice lawlessness, and will cast them into the furnace of fire.

There will be wailing and gnashing of teeth. Then the righteous will shine forth as the sun in the kingdom of their Father. He who has ears to hear, let him hear!'" (Matthew 13:36–43)

Satan is a liar and has no truth in him. He was a murderer from the beginning:

"Ye are of your father the devil, and the lusts of your father ye will do. He was a murderer from the beginning, and abode not in the truth, because there is no truth in him. When he speaketh a lie, he speaketh of his own: for he is a liar, and the father of it." (John 8:44)

Satan sinned from the beginning, while Lucifer was perfect from the day he was created until iniquity was found in him:

"He that committeth sin is of the devil; for the devil sinneth from the beginning. For this purpose the Son of God was manifested, that he might destroy the works of the devil." (1 John 3:8)

Lucifer sinned later on in his existence:

"Thou wast perfect in thy ways from the day that thou wast created, till iniquity was found in thee." (Ezekiel 28:15)

Like I mentioned before, Satan had the power of death. The word came in the flesh and manifested himself as Jesus, so that through death, Jesus might destroy the devil:

"Forasmuch then as the children are partakers of flesh and blood, he [Jesus] also himself likewise took part of the same; that through death he [Jesus] might destroy him [Satan] that had the power of death, that is, the devil." (Hebrews 2:14)

Jesus has all power in heaven and Earth, over all principalities, powers, rulers, and authority. This also includes the devil. Jesus will put all his enemies under his feet.

"Who is gone into heaven, and is on the right hand of God; angels and authorities and powers being made subject unto him." (1 Peter 3:22)

According to the Bible, Jesus (the word of God) made all things:

"For by him were all things created, that are in heaven, and that are in earth, visible and invisible, whether they be thrones, or dominions, or principalities, or powers: all things were created by him, and for him." (Colossians 1:16)

According to scripture, we are in a spiritual warfare not only against Satan, but against powers, principalities, spiritual wickedness in high places, and the rulers of the darkness of this world.

"For we wrestle not against flesh and blood, but against principalities, against powers, against the rulers of the darkness of this world, against spiritual wickedness in high places." (Ephesians 6:12)

Let us look at one of these factors: wickedness. In the Bible, wickedness is portrayed as a woman and has established itself in the land of Shinar, which is modern-day Iraq.

"Then the angel that talked with me went forth, and said unto me, Lift up now thine eyes, and see what is this that goeth forth. And I said, What is it? And he said, This is an ephah that goeth forth. He said moreover, This is their resemblance through all the earth. And, behold, there was lifted up a talent of lead: and this is a woman that sitteth in the midst of the ephah. And he said, This is wickedness. And he cast it into the midst of the ephah; and he cast the weight of lead upon the mouth thereof. Then lifted I up mine eyes, and looked, and, behold, there came out two women, and the wind was in their wings; for they had wings like the wings of a stork: and they lifted up the ephah between the earth and the heaven. Then said I to the angel that talked with me, Whither do these bear the ephah? And he said unto me, To build it an house in the land of Shinar: and it shall be established, and set there upon her own base." (Zechariah 5:5–11)

Satan has power:

"And the LORD said unto Satan, Behold, all that he hath is in thy power; only upon himself put not forth thine hand. So Satan went forth from the presence of the LORD." (Job 1:12)

"And the devil said unto him, All this power will I give thee, and the glory of them: for that is delivered unto me; and to whomsoever I will I give it." (Luke 4:6)

These were the questions that came to mind on this subject. It got my brain going, so I started to connect the dots.

The books of Daniel and Revelation discuss how Satan drew a third of the angels of heaven and cast them to the earth. It then states that Satan stamped upon some of the host of heaven and the angels of God, which he cast to the ground.

"And there appeared another wonder in heaven; and behold a great red dragon [Satan], having seven heads and ten horns, and seven crowns upon his heads.

And his tail drew the third part of the stars of heaven [angels], and did cast them to the earth." (Revelation 12:3–4)

"And it waxed great [Satan], even to the host of heaven [spiritual beings that live in heaven]; and it cast down some of the host [these spiritual beings] and of the stars [angels] to the ground, and stamped upon them." (Daniel 8:10)

This is why God is called "the Lord of Hosts," because he has these spiritual beings that live in heaven; they do God's will. It's not only angels that live in heaven.

"The Lord hath prepared his throne in the heavens; and his kingdom ruleth over all.

Bless the Lord, ye his angels, that excel in strength, that do his commandments, hearkening unto the voice of his word.

Bless ye the Lord, all ye his hosts; ye ministers of his, that do his pleasure.

Bless the Lord, all his works in all places of his dominion: bless the Lord, O my soul." (Psalm 103:19:22)

I will give you an example of the hosts of heaven:

"And he said, Hear thou therefore the word of the Lord: I saw the Lord sitting on his throne, and all the host of heaven standing by him on his right hand and on his left.

And the Lord said, Who shall persuade Ahab, that he may go up and fall at Ramothgilead? And one said on this manner, and another said on that manner.

And there came forth a spirit, and stood before the LORD, and said, I will persuade him.

And the LORD said unto him, Wherewith? And he said, I will go forth, and I will be a lying spirit in the mouth of all his prophets. And he said, Thou shalt persuade him, and prevail also: go forth, and do so.

Now therefore, behold, the LORD hath put a lying spirit in the mouth of all these thy prophets, and the LORD hath spoken evil concerning thee." (1 Kings 22:19–23)

I was looking up scripture about Lucifer and Satan's end, and came across these verses. The first one was about Lucifer. In the Bible, it states:

"By the multitude of thy merchandise they have filled the midst of thee with violence, and thou hast sinned: therefore I will cast thee as profane out of the mountain of God: and I will_destroy thee, O covering cherub, from the midst of the stones of fire. Thou hast defiled thy sanctuaries by the multitude of thine iniquities, by the iniquity of thy traffick; therefore will I bring forth a fire from the midst of thee, it shall devour thee, and I will bring thee to ashes upon the earth in the sight of all them that behold thee. All they that know thee among the people shall be astonished at thee: thou shalt be a terror, and never shalt thou be any more." (Ezekiel 28:16–19)

I then heard an audible voice from a demon say to me, as clear as crystal, "Watch your step." I continued to look at scripture and came across this verse:

"And the devil, who deceived them, was thrown into the lake of burning sulphur, where the beast and the false prophet had been thrown. They will be tormented day and night forever and ever." (Revelation 20:10)

You see, Lucifer ends up being devoured by fire, becoming ashes upon the Earth, never to exist again, while Satan ends up being tormented in the lake of fire for all eternity.

As I was studying this, the same demonic voice returned and said, "I'm going to kill you."

After I arrived home and began to write this all up on the laptop, a spirit entered me, giving me a massive headache. He said, "I'm going to kill you, stop writing this."

Did Satan deceive all the Christians with the doctrine of him being an angel of light: Lucifer? What would Satan's real name be, then? It would not be Lucifer. The names Satan and the devil are just titles given to him. They are not his real name. I am comparing scripture, and the Bible should not contradict itself. I truly believe God has opened my eyes to be able to see this clearly. Can you see it?

I also wonder who filled the midst of Lucifer with violence. We can only wonder if the devil or other powers had something to do with it.

"By the multitude of thy merchandise they have filled the midst of thee with violence, and thou hast sinned." (Ezekiel 28:16)

Joshua and I went to a healing deliverance meeting. A pastor prayed over me. As he was praying, I felt a spirit leave my body, and for a few seconds, I felt slightly delivered. When the pastor prayed over me, he prayed in tongues like my grandmother does, and it sounded familiar. Once he finished praying, he walked away.

As I walked away from the pastor, I heard a voice which sounded like Jesus say to me, "Go and ask the pastor to pray over you again."

It sounded real, and I almost fell for it again. It spoke three times like this, almost convincing me that this was the Lord Jesus talking to me, but I recognised that it was actually a demon. I had to keep reminding myself to test the spirits like the Bible teaches. I still went back to the pastor and asked him to pray over me again. I was so desperate, I needed to get delivered. The realisation hit me hard; I didn't get delivered. I felt a spirit re-enter me.

A lady from the deliverance meeting asked me, "Are you filled with the Holy Spirit?" and I said, "No, I'm not. I'm possessed by an evil spirit which is inside of me."

I know now that I just had unclean spirits dwelling inside and around me; at the time, I didn't understand that I wasn't possessed, even though demons tried to possess me a few times.

At the time, I also didn't know whether I was filled with the Holy Spirit or not. I know the Lord opened my eyes to discernment and gave me some understanding and faith. I'm able to recognise a lot more things now. I believe that I've been given the gift of the Holy Spirit. She tried to show me how to get the infilling of the Holy Spirit, but this scared me, and I left. I'm very hesitant of these things, especially after going through massive amounts of torment. I know you can get a demon which speaks in demonic tongues, and I was scared of getting this. Satan and the demons have hurt me deeply. I believe we should test these spirits. Not every tongue spoken is from the Holy Spirit. You need to test these tongues and ask the spirit directly if the Lord came in the flesh. I believe the spirit can answer you. You may be cursing the Lord if you have tongues from a demon. Test the spirit to make sure it's from the Lord.

I'll give you an example: I was in the car listening to a messianic song that was sung in Hebrew. I didn't know the words to this song, but all of a sudden, I was able to sing this song in Hebrew. I quickly stopped and ask this spirit if the Lord came in the flesh. "Yes, the Lord came in the flesh" was the answer I received. I continued to sing in Hebrew until the song ended.

When I was researching places where I could be delivered, I came upon places where they can teach you how to get the baptism or infilling of the Holy Spirit. Please be careful of such things. God gives these gifts; speaking in tongues is not a sign that you have the Holy Spirit. There are diverse types of gifts that the Lord gives to his children. Speaking in tongues is just one of these gifts. However, this is not a sign that you have the Holy Spirit.

When I got home from the deliverance meeting, I was upset. I started to call out to God and said, "Lord, am I truly one of your children?" I felt completely lost and without hope. I prayed that the Lord would either heal me or take me to heaven because I couldn't take it anymore. I was in agony because of physical and mental torment and sickness.

As I sat at home, I continued to cry. As I was crying, I felt this heat surrounding me. This was the Holy Spirit; as soon as he was around me, he left. I went to my room and prayed with all my heart with more tears. It left me with hope and gave me comfort, knowing that I was indeed a child of God.

A demon spoke and tempted me to re-enter the daydream world. He continued to tell me that I was truly evil due to my past imaginations.

I refused and decided to lie down on the couch; the spirit said, "Just daydream."

I said, "No, I'll never go back into it."

The spirit sent a tingling sexual temptation through my body and continued to say, "Satan wanted you, Danica!"

I didn't question why he said this but quickly replied, "I rebuke you in the name of Jesus," and it left.

One evening, I said sarcastically, "Why doesn't Satan talk to me directly?" I quickly stopped myself in this thought, for I knew it was evil, but it was too late. Suddenly, a male voice came through to me. I covered my face out of shock, for I knew that this was Satan himself speaking directly to me.

I was grieved, and he said, "You are writing something I don't want anyone to know. I warn you: I will get to you. I will kill you." He spoke in a subtle, smooth tone of voice, almost civil in conversation. It was loud and clear, and I knew I had just heard from the devil himself. He didn't say anything else, just these words.

It was a few minutes to midnight, and I got on my knees and started to pray. As I began to pray, something came over me, and I felt this urge to say, "Please forgive me for talking to demons."

I kept getting this urge until I realised it was from the enemy. Instantly, I tried to stop myself from speaking, but my mouth kept opening up. I kept saying in a male tone of voice, "Danica, I am Satan!"

I tried to rebuke it in the name of Jesus, thinking it was just a demon. It continued to speak through me and said, "You can't rebuke me, Danica. I am Satan."

Confused by this, I climbed into bed. As I sat up in bed, Jesus urgently gave me these words: "I am safe and secure in the rock of all ages, and his banner over me is love."

After receiving these words, I suddenly felt this extremely powerful, tingling presence of an evil being standing directly opposite me. At the time, I couldn't tell if this was a demon. However, it was claiming to be Satan himself. I wasn't able to move from the tormenting presence. I saw an outline of him, but the form was invisible. However, I knew he was standing opposite me. This presence alone put fear and torment through my entire body. My whole body tingled with tormenting pain, and I started to feel faint.

The being said, "I'm not going to kill you tonight, but I want you to stop what you are writing." He continued, "I wanted you for a bride, but the Lord wouldn't allow it."

This being lifted his hand over me, and I felt a very powerful sexual desire, which ran right through the lower parts of my body with an intensity that I was almost lured away in a moment of pain and pleasure. I was and wasn't afraid of his presence, for this being gave me mixed signals.

As he was tormenting me, I started to rebuke this being, saying, "I rebuke you in the name of Jesus."

He replied, "You can't rebuke me, Danica. I am Satan."

I was stunned and lay still, unable to breathe, surrounded by an intense feeling of torment. I resisted with all my strength and kept on rebuking, but I wasn't able to get this being to leave me alone. He continued to torment me for a few hours, and then he left.

I was extremely messed up by this. However, I thought I would go on the computer and write this all up before I forgot what happened to me. As soon as I got near the computer, I felt this supernatural pressure on my chest, then I heard these words directed to me:

"I warn you … I will kill you."

Scared by this, I decided to leave it alone for the night. I headed back to bed at 4.30 a.m. and fell asleep.

The next day, I decided to write my experience up, but as soon as I went onto the computer, my head suddenly became compressed with physical pain. I was in extreme agony.

This demon spoke and said, "It's going to get worse, not better, for you."

What else could possibly come my way? I thought.

My head still hurts. I kept on crying out to the Lord for deliverance; I asked him again, "Am I your child?"

He responded instantly to me through this song: "God, You Are Love, for You Saved Me" I was in absolute pain, to the point where I was unable to move from all these attacks that I received.

One day, I was walking home from work, when I started wondering if God would tell me something, anything about what was occurring with my situation. I had great hope that he would give me some sort of answer. I was still working at the Chiropractic clinic.

As I was awaking from sleep one morning, I said, "You were with the devil! You were a disgrace!"

I kept repeating this until I became aware of what I was saying. This was God telling me what a disgrace I was. I felt the rebuke from God, and it deeply hurt. This truly wasn't the answer I wanted to hear, but God wanted me to be aware that I had been on the enemy's side almost my entire life. I was extremely sad and realised just how evil I was. I had joined Satan without even realising that I did. I had come out of his kingdom, and Satan wasn't impressed at all by it.

CHAPTER 12

RESIST

ONE NIGHT, I dreamt that I was wrestling with a black dragon. In this dream, the dragon kept trying to destroy me. As I was dreaming, I cried out to Jesus and said, "Jesus, I love you." Once again, Satan wanted to kill me within a dream. As I woke up, the feeling of death disappeared. If it wasn't for God's presence and everything God has done for me until now, I would believe that I was perishing and going to hell.

Another day, I was at church when my mind for some reason wanted to deny the Lord. I quickly grew angry at myself and kneeled down to pray. Suddenly, the Holy Spirit started to correct me. The Holy Spirit spoke through me and said not to go against the Lord. I got home, and my mind again wanted to deny the Lord. I cried with all my heart and prayed again. The Holy Spirit again corrected me and told me not to go against him. I cried with many tears. I was all upset again.

As I was crying, two songs entered my mind. They were "Unto Thee, Oh Lord" and "A Mighty Fortress Is Our God." I went to the computer to play these songs. I also played "Be Thou My Vision." I started to sing along to this song but couldn't remember the lyrics. As I started to sing, the Lord suddenly gave me the lyrics to this song. I sang it correctly, without getting a single word wrong.

I wrote to Anne again regarding her channel. I tried desperately to reach her but was unable to make her see that she was communicating with a demon. She wouldn't even test this spirit. I told her to try and see who was truly speaking to her by asking this false Jesus if the Lord had come in the flesh. Unfortunately, she trusted this Jesus and was unwilling to listen. She wouldn't take my advice and ask this question.

I told her, "Even if this is Jesus himself, ask this question; he will forgive you if you are truly talking to him."

However, this was a demon she was in communication with. The worse thing is that she has thousands of followers, listening to her on a daily basis. One day, the Lord Jesus spoke to me within my spirit while I was communicating with Anne.

He said, "None of her messages are from the Lord, as well as the visions she gets."

I decided to obey the Lord and wrote his words in the comment section on her videos, even to individual people commenting. Even if she doesn't believe, others can see this and consider. We as Christians should fight for the truth, no matter how crazy you look to others. Just fight for what's right.

I was still being attacked by the unclean spirits. I was in torment one day and grew weak. My mouth locked, and I was just about to swear against the Holy Spirit. Suddenly, the Lord performed a miracle and took over my speech supernaturally. He spoke these particular words through me. He said, "I rebuke you, Satan, in the name of the Lord Jesus." I'm not sure if it was an angel or a spirit from the Lord God. However, it was definitely from the Lord.

I was sitting on the couch and felt this incredible amount of torment hit me hard. I sat there, trying to resist. The demons once again wanted me to curse the Holy Spirit. Out of the blue, a male voice spoke to me. It was an angel of light. He gives me these words: "Resist, and you'll receive a crown of life."

The spirits I've encountered so far have a lot of character. Some sound demonic, but others don't. They seem to have their own personality. Even the way they speak, you can't believe that it's your mind coming up with such comments. They are not even connected to your own thoughts. Flowing thoughts are not connected to your mind. They either come from the Lord, from demons, or from Satan, depending on what you get.

This is why a lot of people say, "I have that song stuck in my head." If you receive a song or thought from the devil or demons, rebuke them immediately in the name of Jesus, and the spirit giving you this thought should stop. I've done this a number of times already regarding songs that have entered my mind from the devil. When I notice this, I immediately rebuke it in the name of the Lord.

"They are trying to lure you away from me," God our Father told me one day.

I thought, *This could never happen to me because I love the Lord very much.*

Soon after I received these words, the worst temptation I ever had happened to me. I was asleep and went into a very realistic dream. I couldn't tell the difference between the dream world and reality for a few minutes. I was overwhelmed by a demon. I felt this demon's hand inside my private parts. As I felt the hand there, I had this unbelievably strong desire to worship Satan. It was 3 a.m. I got up and took a hot bath to stop myself from worshipping him. It was the worse evil desire that I ever had. They could have lured me away with the way I felt. This desire they placed on me was unbearable, to the point where I could have fallen for it. I had to resist this urge and remember that I was a Christian, and that Satan and the demons are darkness, and that we are the children of light.

"Submit yourselves therefore to God. Resist the devil and he will flee from you." (James 4:7)

While sitting in the bath, I received this song from the Lord: "I Serve a Risen Saviour." The song gave me strength to resist Satan. The feeling subsided, and the unclean spirits started to speak to me again. They kept telling me they just wanted me to go to hell.

One horrible night, I was dreaming when all of a sudden my

dream shifted. Satan took control of my dream. While in this dream state, I called the Holy Spirit an evil spirit.

I heard Satan's voice within this dream; he said, "You're going to hell."

I replied back to him in disappointment, "I had a feeling I was."

My whole body woke up in extreme anger over this. Satan had put it in my heart to try to blaspheme God. Thinking I was doomed eternally, I sat up in bed, unable to control just how annoyed and frustrated I was about saying these words. I thought I had just blasphemed God. I had hatred within me; I almost cursed God. I sat up in bed, holding it all back, almost unable to control it. However, I didn't curse God, and the anger and hatred towards God left me. I resisted Satan, and the feeling fled. I can't believe that Satan can control your emotions like this. I was overwhelmed and didn't know what to do. I just had to believe the Lord was saving me. I didn't do this willingly. It was against my will. Satan directed my thoughts to the Holy Spirit, to refer to him as an evil spirit. I'm crying now; I can't believe the devil is able to do such a thing to a Christian.

I thought I was wearing a helmet. My head felt heavy, and I was in constant agony. I finally decided to go to the local medical centre for an answer. I arrived, waited, and was eventually seen by a doctor. She heard my case and sent me to the hospital for a more thorough investigation.

As Joshua and I ended up back at the emergency ward at the hospital, torment started to race through my mind. Unable to cope, I put on my iPod and played Christian instrumental music to soothe my thoughts. I couldn't take it anymore. The torment wasn't just mental; it was also physical. I was pushed to my breaking point, with high levels of stress for over six months. That was how long I had been resisting Satan with evil thoughts against the Holy Spirit. I cried nearly every night for deliverance, unable to bear the tormenting pain that inflicted me. I had great hope that the Lord would answer my prayers one day.

I was finally admitted and seen by the doctors. They did a CT scan to check my brain, and the results came back; it was the same as my CT scans from our holiday: all clear. When they told me that I was clear, my compressions inside my brain increased, and my physical and mental torment grew worse. I believe that demons were causing me these compressions.

When we left the hospital, I was in more agony, physically as well as mentally, than when I arrived. However, there was nothing else they could do for me. I ended up leaving and went to Tina and Andrew's to pick up the children. In tears, I turned to the Lord. I couldn't sit down. I was completely agitated, to the point where I wanted to pull my hair out. I paced up and down, unable to find rest.

As I kneeled to pray, I called out to the Lord and asked him to help me for my children's sake. I didn't want to lose custody of them due to my sickness. Instantly, he settled me, taking away the physical and mental torment during prayer. I was so relieved and quickly turned to my brother-in-law, Daniel, and told him that the Lord just healed me from torment. He didn't know what to say back to me. He didn't understand what I was really going through. However, this started my road to recovery.

CHAPTER 13

UNDISCIPLINED

MY CHILDREN AND I were all cuddled up together in my bed. We just sang a song to the Lord, and then "I will deliver you" came through my mouth. This was the second time I was told I'd be delivered. Just before I got these words, I was in prayer, and "I love you" came through my mouth. This was the Lord God telling me that he loved me and that he'd deliver me.

While I was lying in bed, I began to supernaturally hear Christians singing a song of praise to God. As soon as I started to listen to them, Satan intervened by placing an awful sound to block the incoming music. I was annoyed; I really wanted to hear what the Lord was showing me. I felt extremely angry when Satan blocked the music.

Violet attends a Christian school. She had a school performance one evening, and it was a major production. We went to the school and were directed to our seats. The students were getting ready to play their instruments. All the parents were seated, and we waited for the curtains to open. All I knew about the performance was that my child was to sing a song with her class on stage.

When they opened, the theme was Broadway musical; I was in shock. This was a Christian school. I was upset as I sat there, watching my child perform to the music. I was grieved and thought, *I wonder if the Lord can make me sick so I can leave?*

I took it back straight away, regretting what I just said, but I got instantly sick and felt a pain in my abdomen. I also felt the Lord's presence; he told me to leave my seat and go outside. The Lord wasn't happy at all with the situation. As the Lord was directing me to leave, a Christian student started to perform a song from a popular Broadway musical regarding witches. I quickly got up and went outside, walking out in pain. I had offended Joshua by leaving, but I obeyed the Lord and left my seat. I wonder why a lot of Christians are involved heavily with the world like this; the Lord doesn't like it.

The truth is, Satan is a roaring lion and wants to devour everyone. He uses tools like books, movies, music and entertainment to draw people away from the Lord. Some of these popular children's books teach our children to love wizardry, sorcery and evil. Through these types of books, children learn about the occult. The worst thing is, Christian parents are allowing their children to read them. As a result, Satan is given the legal right to enter into their lives, along with demons. One time during book week, a teacher at Violet's school picked a student to win best dressed out of his school grade. These students all came dressed as their favourite characters from their favourite books. This student that won best dress, was dressed as a young wizard. I was so angry. I watched how Christian parents clapped their hands together and supported this abomination. You can't serve Satan and Jesus at the same time. You need to choose who you want to serve. We as Christians need to stay away from such things and try to live a righteous life.

However, I'm still learning to live a righteous life. I want to confess a few things about my attitude towards unclean spirits. The spirits speak to me most of the time, and I'm sometimes tempted by them. They try to lure me into a conversation. Even though most times, I refuse to speak back to them, I end up listening and smile stupidly about what the spirits have to say. I'm getting better; at least I'm no longer grinning in awe about hearing a spirit. I am now grieved by them. I truly want it to all stop. I pray to the Lord that he can deliver me from them. They just won't leave.

One day, while praying to the Lord, he told me, "Do a three-day fast."

Three days? I cringed inside, knowing full well how hard it would be for me to achieve this. However, I was determined to do this for the Lord. I started but crumbled again and again, until I gave up fasting completely. *I just can't do it*, I told myself in disappointment. I love the Lord, but I just can't get through the fast. I kept failing. I even vowed to the Lord that I would do this for him. I know, don't vow unless you really mean it. God hates it when you go back on your word. At the time of the vow, I really wanted to do this for God, but my body wasn't able to fast that long.

After I failed this fast, I heard these words come to me: "I will not deliver you." I thought it was the Lord at first, but it happened so fast that to this day, I'm not sure if it was God who spoke or a demon. I became sad and was unsure if I would get delivered. I really lost hope that God would deliver me from the demons.

After this, my family and I went to the shopping centre. Joshua and I sat down and let the children play in the indoor playground. As I sat down, a spirit began to communicate with me. As I was listening to the demon, I accidently said something that I knew wasn't pleasing to the Lord. As soon as these words entered my mind (it had something to do with the Holy Spirit), I felt this presence of wrath come upon me. I sat there on the seat, stunned, unable to speak, for I felt doomed. After the initial shock, I started to cry in public. It felt like God was warning me.

We arrived home, and tears were still coming down my face. Why did I say this? I was so sad, and depression started to set in. My mouth suddenly opened up, and a male voice spoke through me and said, "I am saved."

I raced off to church, against Joshua's wishes. I just had to leave. As I sat in the church, I felt God's presence helping me sing a hymn again. I cried all through the service and then went home, still feeling uneasy.

That night, I felt the urge to go and pray. I got up and started praying, when out of nowhere, a powerful male voice spoke directly through me. He said, "You will never be saved."

I trembled in panic and started to cry uncontrollably.

The powerful voice that spoke these words took over my mouth; it repeated forcefully, "You will never be saved."

An eternally lost feeling came over me again. As I continued to cry, I heard another male spirit say, "Please believe that you are saved. Don't believe a lie."

It was too late; the damage was done. I was in fear of being lost. My whole body trembled at the thought of being lost forever. I cried with all my heart, grieved at the thought. As I lay on the bed, I received this song: "When We All Get to Heaven." It gave me comfort, but I was still in tears from such an attack. It brought fear to my soul and grieved me to the core.

The next morning, I sat on the kitchen chair and said to the Lord out loud, "I am not right." I continued, "Why did I have to go through all of this?"

Suddenly, I felt the Lord's presence come upon me. He spoke through me and said, "I will save your soul."

I quickly got on my knees and cried out with thanks to our God. I was saved. I couldn't believe it. After everything I'd done against God, he still saved me by his grace and mercy.

A few days later, I began to feel the torment again, as wicked flowing thoughts started to come into my mind against the Holy Spirit. I ended up pacing up and down the corridor in distress. The enemy was once again putting evil thoughts inside my mind, and I had to resist it. As I was pacing, I suddenly felt this very powerful spirit enter me. It tried hard to possess me.

I straight away panicked and said, "I rebuke you in the name of Jesus."

The spirit pulled out straight away and left me. It was amazing to see how spirits leave in the name of Jesus. His name is powerful.

The Lord started to hold me together. The evil thoughts that Satan and the demons were giving me stopped. My mind was clear.

I could feel the Lord grabbing each thought that entered my mind and taking them away supernaturally. My stress levels also decreased. I still longed for deliverance from the demons, as well as healing of the physical pain that affected my body. The demons, however, still wanted me to interact with them, whether in a dream or while I was awake. They kept on trying to lure me over to Satan.

Over the next two days, I was lured away again. The spirits continuously talked to me all day long, for two days straight. My heart started to become drawn away from the Lord due to the constant interaction I received from these beings. *What's wrong with me?* I thought. The feeling of disappointment sunk deep inside my mind. I was a disappointment to the Lord, and I knew I was sinning. I was unable to bring myself to face the Lord, out of fear of being rebuked by him.

That night, I quickly rushed through my prayers and hopped straight into bed. I just could not face him. As I went into a deep sleep, the Lord spoke to me and said, "I don't want to put you into the lake of fire. I love you." He spoke to me as if I was one of his little children.

His love lingered inside my heart, and the most incredible, comforting feeling surrounded me. I woke up out of sleep and felt loved by the Lord. I quickly felt bad and repented what I'd done for the last two days. The demons just wanted to lure me away from God.

The love of the Father is incredible, and it touched me deeply. "Loved by God," I pondered. How incredible is this? As I started to sing "Amazing Grace," I felt the Lord's presence with me through song, and I just knew he loved me as his child.

On another day, I was considering the covenant that the Lord gave me, as well as the prophecy that the Lord gave to my grandfather about saving us. The Lord spoke to me in surprise and said that I could still go to hell. He was just informing me that it was still possible for me to end up there. I took note as he advised me of this. He wasn't trying to scare me, but this is a warning to all:

Christians can go to hell. Some Christians believe in the doctrine of "once saved, always saved." This is a lie. Be very careful of such teachings.

"Not everyone who says to me, 'Lord, Lord,' will enter into the Kingdom of Heaven; but he who does the will of my Father who is in heaven." (Matthew 7:21)

CHAPTER 14

DELIVERANCE

There is a book I really recommend everyone to read: *He Came to Set the Captives Free,* by Rebecca Brown MD. It's a very interesting book. I believe the testimony and agree with nearly everything that Rebecca wrote. I see her as a genuine Christian who went through a lot of things in her life and is truly hearing from the Lord. The book is about a doctor who helped a woman named Elaine come out of Satanism and dedicate her life to Jesus. Elaine was a witch in Satan's kingdom. When she left Satanism, the demons turned against her and attacked her. I won't give too much away regarding her story. Dr. Brown has written a few other books. *Prepare for War* and *Becoming a Vessel of Honor* are another two good books to read.

I searched the Internet for another deliverance service and found a church that was hosting one. The man they invited was a healing evangelist. He worked as a missionary pastor with the Aboriginal tribal people. He saw how the tribal witch doctors had power, so he cried out to the Lord with prayer and fasting until the Lord started to work with him. Healing started to take place among the people, and miracles happened. He is now working full time for the Lord, travelling in Australia and also going overseas to set people free from various sicknesses. It sounded promising, and I wondered if God would deliver me if I went to it.

His arrival to my city was set for October 30, 2016. I wanted to meet this man and see if God would finally set me free. I asked my father and Lisa to come with me, but she wasn't convinced that he was working for the Lord and told me not to go to see this man, but I believe the Lord can work through people. Also, his testimony sounded genuine.

The three-day fast still lingered inside my mind. I had to do another fast before the healing service. I just had to do it for the Lord. Even if he didn't deliver me this time, I said to myself, I wouldn't get upset. God has his reasons why some people get delivered and others don't.

The evil spirits started to grieve me again against the Holy Spirit. I was so tired of it now and begged the Lord not to let me go. He was still holding my own thoughts in place. I was so scared to blaspheme and didn't want to return to the torment I went through with the demons. I was drained to the point that I wanted the Lord to take me away from this world. I was afraid I'd blaspheme against him and not enter into the kingdom of heaven. He gave me a quick no in my spirit, and I knew I wasn't going to die anytime soon.

"I want to live," I told the Lord, but I couldn't live in torment. I was recovering from the attacks, but somehow Satan was determined to get me into hell by sinning greatly against God. The Lord, however, wasn't allowing him to completely destroy me. The Lord told me one time during prayer that "I have forgiven you, and I will have mercy on you."

I began the fast but failed again. I just couldn't do it. I was unable to fast for the required length of time. I stopped and wondered if I would ever achieve a long fast again.

My heart became wicked again. I spoke some evil words out loud, and this time, the Lord spoke powerfully through me; he said, "I will save your soul, but if you continue the way you are going, I will not."

I was shocked. I was rebuked with a stern warning and was afraid for my soul. This old me had to go; I cannot even write down what I said. It was something I never want to repeat again. It was enough for the Lord to speak directly through me with this warning.

I spoke in faith and told Satan a few things about never going back to him and never again falling for his traps. I was upset and felt my whole life was a big mess because of what Satan had done to me as a young child, by luring into this dark, demonic dream world. When I entered into this world, I completely left the Lord behind. However, while I daydreamed, I always wondered why my fantasy world wasn't even darker. I always thought someone was watching me. Now I know it was the Lord. I grieved him for twenty-two years through my imagination.

I was again tormented by my own thoughts against the Holy Spirit. I didn't get hardly any sleep. I stayed up and prayed for over three hours straight. At the end of my prayer, the Lord's presence came around me. I stopped praying and asked God if he would deliver me tomorrow at the service, and he said no in my spirit. I accepted this; however, I still wanted to go to the healing service, just in case God surprised me.

I was in physical pain; my hands felt a tingling, swelling sensation, while my head, back, and neck had compressed pain. I also asked him a few other questions; his presence was still around me. I was extremely happy because the Lord was speaking to me directly through my spirit. I also asked him if he would send someone to heal me, and he again said no.

I arrived at my father's place shortly before eight o'clock. I was tired due to lack of sleep, and he offered to make me a coffee. I told him I had one earlier. I patiently waited for him to leave for the church service. We drove for about forty minutes to the church hosting the healing service. We went upstairs and took our seats. The service began with singing and praise to our Lord, then a pastor introduced the guest healing evangelist. He started to call out people's conditions, and they went out to the front for direct prayer. Most of them claimed some type of healing, and I went up and told him I had compression in my neck, head, and back, as well as schizophrenia. He put his hand on my neck, and I felt the compression go away instantly; my hands stopped the tingling sensation also. I still could hear the demons speaking to me, for I was not delivered from them. The Lord did say within my spirit that I wouldn't get delivered that day.

As I walked back to my seat, the physical pain got worse. I wondered if I truly got healed in the first place; as I pondered this, I felt the Lord heal the pain in these areas completely. The service ended, and I walked silently down to the car, thinking, *Did I really just get healed?*

I arrived home and told Joshua, "God healed me physically from the pain."

His response was, "Whatever makes you feel better."

What an odd response from my husband. I quickly realised that he didn't understand what the healing power of God can do in a person's life. However, the Lord was right. He said I would not be delivered today. I decided to lay down, and for the first time in a long time, I felt at ease.

Shortly after I was healed from the physical pain, the demons began to put pain back inside my body. They didn't make it easy for me. They brought back the torment. In tears, I cried out to God with all my heart to help me. I couldn't go through anymore torment; I had enough. God's presence came into the room. I quickly asked the Lord if he could send an angel to protect me from the demons. The Lord agreed and told me within my spirit that he would. As soon as he agreed, I instantly felt at peace and the torment ceased straight away. He quickly answered my prayer, and I was very relieved that he did.

I was praying to God, when his presence once again entered into the room. I said out loud to the Lord, "I haven't heard from Jesus for a long time."

I continued to ponder; I wondered if I should ask God for a word through one of his prophetess that I knew of since my childhood. However, he read my mind and gently asked me not to. I didn't know why he didn't want me to ask him this question. However, I obeyed his request and didn't ask the Lord. Somehow, I drifted off to sleep. I found myself within a dream, when suddenly I was awakened by a gentle touch from our Lord Jesus Christ. I saw him in the spirit. I knew it was the Lord Jesus because his presence told me it was him. The Lord Jesus must have heard what I had said earlier to our heavenly Father. It was an incredible experience and an honour to see the Lord Jesus this way. I'm in awe of our Lord.

I finally started to exercise, which I found amazing because I thought I would never recover from the sickness. I was starting to return to my normal self. A lot had to do with the Lord helping me, as well as the antipsychotic medication I was taking. The Lord was giving me some peace and the ability to cope again. I also needed to get fit again. I used to be pretty fit and weighed in around sixty kilograms before having my second child. I wanted to return back to my normal self in that perspective but found it hard to. The demons were still around me. They kept on telling me how much they wanted me to lose weight, even requesting to be my personal trainer or possess me to help me lose the weight. They wanted me to willingly surrender my will to them and let them take over me. I also refused this. I didn't want to be possessed. As I was in the middle of a fitness video, a demon entered into me. He started to help me perform better. I didn't feel possessed, but I knew it was in me. My performance level increased to a much higher level of fitness. I stopped when I noticed this and rebuked the demon. He sent a sexual temptation through my body and then left.

CHAPTER 15

THE DEVIL

"YOU ARE WELCOME to come back anytime," an invitation was offered to me. The voice that spoke was smooth and subtle, almost fooling me into thinking that the devil himself had spoken directly to me. It is hard to distinguish when demons portray themselves as the devil. You can easily believe that the devil himself had spoken directly to you. However, this being was telling me that he wanted me to return back to the world of daydreaming. I'll never return to that world willingly; I'll never watch another demonic-inspired film or series or read another novel that isn't Christian. You also have to be careful with some Christian books, for not everyone who claims to be a Christian is truly one.

I want to warn anyone else who is imagining like I did to think twice before doing so. For you are for Satan and doing his will and not God's will. Any maladaptive daydreamers out there, please consider your ways and do what I did and shut down your worlds. You could end up in hell for it. To all parents, watch your children and teenagers; if they are spending countless hours in a stationary state, listening to music, whether Christian or secular music, then they might be in the world of daydreaming. I know it sounds like nothing, but I'm telling you out of my own personal experience, while within this world, Satan will take advantage of your children's imaginations. He did it to me, and he will do it to your children. I don't know how many people out there truly dream the way I did. However, keep both eyes open and talk to your children about their fantasy lives. They might get a shock when you ask them about it. I know I would've if someone asked me about my deep, dark secret.

I started to write poetry to get my own thoughts off cursing God. I find if I get my mind focussed on something else, it's easier to cope. You see, I have a problem now. I'm constantly afraid that I'm going to blaspheme the Holy Spirit. I'm in fear over it. I keep asking God to help me through the aftermath of the torment. God is my counsellor. He stops me in my tracks from speaking against him. As I was writing this poem, the Lord suddenly gave me a few words to add. The words the Lord gave me are highlighted in bold. I thought I would share this with you:

The wide and the narrow:
Two roads you can take.
Make up your minds
before it's too late.
The wide is the road that leads to hell.
Unwilling to believe,
unwilling to dwell,
to dwell in our Lord
who died on the cross.
Those who believe in him
will never be lost.
Christ Jesus,
our risen King,
is the ruler of all,
in victory through death.
So we are all called
out of darkness into his marvellous light
that we might find the narrow road
and leave this sinful world behind.

I know Christians have mixed views when they talk about the topic of hell. Most Christians believe that hell exists, but a few believe in annihilation, which is not taught in the Bible (except in Lucifer's case). I recommend a book called *23 Minutes in Hell.* It is written by Bill Wiese. He is a Christian brother who was sent to hell by the Lord to bring back a message to the world: that hell is a real place and that Jesus doesn't want anyone to go there.

A while back, I was reading a Christian book (by Rebecca Brown M.D) regarding a woman who was one of Satan's brides. In this book, I read how Satan's bride was involved with the devil in a sexual way. Instantly, I had perversion enter my body. I had to put the book down and didn't read it for a few weeks. One day, I asked the Lord if he wanted me to continue reading this book, and he told me yes within my spirit. I obeyed and continued reading.

I had to ask the Lord this question because this is what he rebuked me for that day I spoke evil. I know I said I won't repeat what I said to anyone, but I think I need to write it down because it shows you my heart at the time and why the Lord rebuked me so much. Please try to forgive me for saying this. I really didn't want to add this in my book. I said, referring to the devil and his bride, "At least she got to experience this."

God rebuked me as soon as these words came out of my mouth. I did ask him if he was God, and he said yes back to me. I just knew it was the Lord. You can't confuse it when you get rebuked like this from God. However, I also noticed that Satan drew me to say these words. The way he drew me was subtle, and I knew it wasn't just me saying it. I felt possessed for a moment. This was the same feeling I felt when I said I wanted to challenge Satan. However, I was afraid to continue reading this book after getting rebuked by God. For some reason, the Lord wanted me to read the rest of it.

One evening, I happened to be sitting at the computer, when suddenly a tormenting tingling presence surrounded me. The skin on my face tightened. Satan was again portrayed to me. He spoke and said, "I wanted you to be my bride." The evil being continued, "I want you to have sex with me."

This being once again put a rush of sexual pleasure throughout my body. I flatly refused his offer, and he quickly left. This temptation probably had a lot to do with the comment I made. Satan is a tempter and a master at that, but was this being truly him? I still believe this was a demon masking itself as Satan.

I decided to go to sleep and found myself within a dream. I dreamt I was on this dark path when Satan suddenly stood in front of me. I can't tell you if this was truly Satan himself or a demon. However, this was what happened. He started to talk to me and introduced the topic of sex. I quickly told him that it was boring and I wanted what the Lord was offering me. I continued to tell him, "I didn't want to miss out on eternity with the Lord Jesus."

When I said these words, this incredible, overwhelming feeling of love entered my body. It was the Lord Jesus who was giving me this incredible feeling. I was filled with such peace. After this conversation, Satan disappeared. The scene changed, and I found myself in the arms of a demon high in the air. He threatened to drop me to the ground; out of fear, I quickly told him not to drop me. I woke up out of sleep and instantly heard a demon tell me, "Satan doesn't want his kingdom to end. The Lord's going to put a stop to it."

Just after this demon spoke, the Lord quickly sent me a song. The song was "Take My Hand, Lord Jesus." I drifted back to sleep and instantly fell back into the dream word. The Lord decided to do something to block me from dreaming. He gave me Christian songs throughout the night. They were loud and clear like a recording. The last song he gave me was "I'm So Glad Jesus Set Me Free." When I awoke out of sleep, I was in such a happy mood. Peace and love lingered inside my heart once again.

I decided to ask the Lord if Satan really did come and tempt me, but I got no answer from him. I asked him a bit later on if Satan really wanted me as one of his brides. He also didn't answer me on this subject. I truly believe this was a lie from the devil. He is a liar and the father of lies. I just believe he wants to devour me, but I still wonder why he's trying to lure me over to him.

I was in a state of sleep and started to dream again. I was talking within this dream about something; I can't remember what I said exactly, but I heard the loudest bang in the ceiling. It was the Lord, and he told me no within my spirit. He was grieved with me. He wanted me to wake up from sleep due to the way I was speaking. I arose straight away and left the dream behind.

I went to bed around two o'clock and quickly drifted into a dream. I suddenly found myself standing before an evil creature. He appeared in the human form, but he was not pleasant to look at. I also was naked before him. This creature, who called himself the Father, licked my body in a horrific way and placed me on a bed. He silently informed me that his son was going to have sex with me. While in this dream, I felt this supernatural sexual desire rising throughout my body. The demons once again were placing this sexual sensation inside of me. Suddenly, I woke up in a frantic mess.

A demon came to me and masked itself as Satan. He said, "I gave you this dream." He continued, "You referred to the Father." He was referring to our heavenly Father.

I answered back and said, "I did not!"

This demon then said, "The tingling sexual desire will take several minutes to stop."

I could still feel this sexual desire rising inside of me. During the conversation, the Lord gave me a song. I had to apologise to him for being in such an awful dream. I really didn't want to go to sleep anymore. I always ended up conversing with demon within my dreams. This demon left, and another started to speak to me.

He said, "If you continue the dream, then we know you want this."

I was grieved and distressed; I was almost lured away by sex because of the sexual desire that was placed inside my body. I decided to get out of bed and stay awake. In the past, I've had dreams where I've tasted sweet and sour lollies and other types of food from demons within a dream. These tastes would linger on my tongue. I really didn't understand why the enemy did this.

The next day, I decided to call Grandmother May. As I was on the phone to her, she all of a sudden mentioned this prophetess the Lord God Almighty told me not to seek a prophecy from. My grandmother wanted to speak to this prophetess regarding me, to see if the Lord would send her a word. I told her that the Lord didn't want me to ask him for a word through her. I did, however, want to know what was happening with my situation; deep down, I wanted something more solid from the Lord, and she had a good reputation. My grandmother, however, still wanted to ask this woman for a word. I told her don't worry, trying to be obedient to the Lord, since he told me not to ask her.

As I finished up at work, my health suddenly declined. I felt like death again. I walked to the train station from the clinic, carrying myself in this state. I felt like falling down onto the ground. As I was waiting to catch the train home, I felt the illness throughout my body. I knew demons were once again giving me physical pain. My head all of a sudden got compressed with pain, and I once again cried out to the Lord for help. As I stood at the station, waiting for the train to arrive, I started to hum a tune quietly to myself, but then the Lord changed the tune. "Day by day, with each new passing moment," came out of my mouth instead.

The feeling of death subsided, and I felt slightly better, but not completely set free from the physical pain. I ask the Lord, "Please take me home." I just couldn't handle any more pain. I was stuck in the middle of a spiritual battle. I started thinking about my children. *Will I die from this?* I thought.

I wanted to see my children grow up, but at the same time, I wanted to depart to the Lord. This sickness was truly killing me inside.

I'm not going back to hospital, I thought. I didn't think they could do anything else for my situation. They probably wouldn't be able to detect a thing, anyway. Tired from all the pain, I decide to do the usual evening routine and took a hot relaxing bath. I wanted to see just how bad my situation would progress first.

After I fell asleep that night, I dreamt I was in my old high school. My old English teacher handed me a book. It was supernatural themed and had a demon on the front cover. I got mad and told him I didn't want to read it and stood up for the Lord, when all of a sudden, I heard my phone ringing. It was my husband, waking me up for work. I had just slept in and quickly had a shower and got dressed, trying to make up lost time. I got my children in the car and headed to my in-laws' place to drop them off. I felt incredible. Yesterday, I felt like death. Today, I had fully recovered and was joyful and glad. I started to write a poem on the train:

> You died on the cross for sinners like me,
> a death as cruel as this.
> In agony, you hung on that tree,
> ridiculed and mocked by your people.
> They put you to shame.
> They saw your good deeds.
> You healed the sick and the lame.
> The ground shook, and the rocks rent.
> The veil was torn in two.
> Christ Jesus had just died
> for sinners just like you.
> What did you do wrong, my King?
> You're a lamb without spot.
> But they cast lots for your cloak and pierced your side
> as they cruelly watched you die.
> Three days did you lie in a tomb,
> but death couldn't hold you.
> In victory you rose and conquered the grave,
> that by you many would come to be saved.

I was happy at work until I heard this: "I am the devil … devil! Yes, Danica. I am the devil." He kept saying these words as he reinforced me that he was indeed the devil.

I kept telling him, "I don't believe that you are. You're a demon."

He got angry at me; he grabbed my body internally and squeezed me and said again, "I am the devil." He continued to speak to me and told me, "I want to kill you." He again reinforced it and said once again, "Yes, I really am the devil."

He sent a sexual temptation through my body and then told me he wanted me to go to hell. He left me, and my day declined; suddenly, I was again resisting these incoming thoughts. I spent the rest of the day resisting thoughts about Satan (I didn't want to serve him). I was all over the place again and couldn't wait for the day to be over with. I went home and typed up everything, as I cried out to the Lord. He once again settled me. I told him I didn't want to leave him for Satan.

I decide to call Grandmother May. I asked her if she got a word from the Lord from this prophetess. She said, "Yes, she got these chapters from Isaiah: 42, 43, and 44. The Lord spoke to her and gave her these chapters."

I read these chapters, and God talks about how he is God and there is no other. He also said how he has blotted out my sin like a thick cloud and how he was going to start a new thing. It reads not to be afraid, that the Lord was with me, that he wasn't going to cast me aside. These chapters really touched me a lot, and I could hear God's voice speaking through these chapters to me, as if he was directly talking to me. I still didn't understand why he didn't want me to ask the prophetess for a word. However, God heard the desires of my heart and gave me something to comfort me. I was very happy when I received these chapters.

Joshua bought us tickets to go to the circus. We got ready to go with our two children. We arrived just before 6 p.m. and took our seats. The music started up, and I got frustrated. I forgot that the circus played secular music. I truly wanted to leave before it started.

The secular music really affected me now. I just couldn't handle it at all. The demons started to talk to me, and I started rebuking them. However, they kept on saying, "You can't rebuke us. You're willing to come into Satan's den." They really didn't leave. They continued to speak to me.

The circus started, and I decided to walk out almost halfway through the show. I took a long walk around the grounds and decided to go back inside to get the car keys and my mobile phone and then sit in the car. Joshua became upset, and I ended up staying at the show. As I took my seat, the demons started to talk to me again. I suddenly felt this very powerful presence next to me. It truly felt like Satan was sitting right next to me. He was in an invisible human form, but I could see him.

He started to talk to me. However, I just kept on resisting him. He stopped speaking to me. The expression across his face said it all. He was extremely annoyed at me. He had this look of silent anger on his face. He told me he was the devil. I kept on proclaiming to him that I wanted to serve my Lord Jesus. I didn't want to serve the devil. After that, he vanished into thin air. Suddenly, I felt this urge inside my mind. The urge was pulling me to worship Satan again. I resisted with all my strength while I was sitting in my seat. I kept on saying, "I serve the living God, and Jesus is my King."

As I was proclaiming these words, I felt God pulling me out of this loop. I was a mess and extremely tired. The circus ended, and we went out for dinner. I was sitting down when a spirit re-entered into me, and the urge returned. I again resisted this supernatural mental anguish. I finally came to a point where I was able to stop myself and just proclaim that Jesus is my King. It was a spiritual battle beyond understanding. I can't explain how a simple flowing thought could make you almost insane. This was what they were doing to me.

I arrived home and quickly rushed to my knees. As I was praying, my mouth suddenly opened up. I thought I had gotten a word from God. (It was hard to recognise whether this word was the Lord or not). I stopped my mouth and asked this spirit who he was.

He responded to me and said he was God. I continued to ask him who he was.

He then said, "I am Satan." He talked through me and said, "I am the devil." He continued, "I am going to kill you."

This was a power voice which spoke clearly and loudly through me. I kept on interrupting him while he spoke. He informed me that he could speak through anyone he chose. I was drained by all the attacks; I couldn't care anymore. I believe that I have a shield of faith and the Lord on my side. After he spoke through me, the Lord sent me a song. It was "Onward, Christian Soldiers." I could hear this inside my mind like a recording.

My friend called me one day and said that she was having suicidal thoughts. I told her that she would go to hell if she killed herself. I told her to cry out to the Lord and to seek him with prayer and fasting. The Lord had come to my aid many times before. After our conversation, I decided to fast for her. As soon as I decided to take up a fast, the Lord instantly gave me three songs in a row, almost telling me to do this for her. Lisa called me back, and I told her to ask the church to take up a fast. She replied that the church didn't believe that true born-again Christians could have a demon inside of them.

I told her, "Yes, they can; both of us are going through this."

Eventually, our church fasted for the two of us. They arranged people to fast for us throughout the week.

As I was fasting for my friend, demons started to compress my entire body. They wanted me to stop fasting for her. I decided to push on instead, wrestling with the spirits around me. My body suddenly became heavy, with pressure which went through my head and chest. I felt this presence, and again I heard a voice speaking to me.

He said, "I am the Devil."

I again said, "You're a demon."

He again repeated that he was indeed the devil. He started to communicate to me and said, "I'm going to kill you in an occult ritual. You'll see what I have installed."

Out of nowhere, my thoughts were drawn to praise the devil. God's wrath suddenly fell over me. God quickly stopped me from worshipping Satan. I resisted and quickly proclaimed that I would kneel only to Jesus.

He said, "I want you to stop fasting. I want your friend to die as badly as I want you dead."

However, I refused. This demon was very close to me physically, for his presence was almost touching my body. After he spoke, he suddenly disappeared.

I was on the surface of sleep when I started to come up with an evil storyline within a dream. As I was inside the dream, two spirits approached me and wanted me to stop the dream. I asked them while still in this dreaming state whether they were from the Lord. They replied back to me and said, "Yes."

This happened a number of times where I thought the Lord stopped me this way by sending a spirit that was working for him. As I went for a shower, one of these spirits started to talk to me; he spoke about my daydream world and said, "Yes, Satan was the one controlling this world." He continued, "It was the first time you took control of your own life, when you repented. You fell away, though. Satan is luring you again in this dream world."

I asked him if the Lord came in the flesh; he said, "Yes, and I'm working for the Lord Jesus," and then they disappeared.

I started asking the Lord to close the doorway to the spirit world. I didn't want this in my life anymore. What did I get involved in? This was how blind I was: I had willingly entered the dream world for almost twenty-two years through my imagination, and now I was dreaming almost every single night and being taunted by demons.

I was again asleep when suddenly, an evil presence grabbed my arm in reality, waking me up. It tried hard to frighten me with fear. It was meant to be Satan himself, but I knew instantly after the attack that this was a demon.

I yelled at him, "I worship Jesus," and then added, "You're weak! Your kingdom has crumbled. Jesus has destroyed it."

I wasn't scared at all. I fought hard against this demon until it let me go and stepped back in a distance.

He began to speak to me and said, "You're not even afraid, are you?"

The Lord tells us in his word that perfect love casts out fear. This was how I felt now. However, I also knew demons can put you through absolute fear. When I was in the mental health facility, I was suddenly woken by a feeling of pure fear. I was lying still on my bed when I felt this feeling surrounding me. It was chilling and went straight through me. I quickly got up and prayed to the Lord on my knees until this feeling fled.

Over time, I noticed that the Lord was delivering me from the unclean spirits. The compressed pain in my head was healed. *No more compression*, I thought, until yesterday. I was on the computer, typing away, trying to completing the Antichrist study in chapter 16, when I had a demon enter into me again, and my compression returned. I was all upset again. I thought I had fully recovered. I asked the Lord if he could once again take out these demons that were causing this particular pain. I was crying again to the Lord, unable to bear the pain inside my head.

I'm back to square one, I thought. The next morning, when I awoke, my head was clear again. The demons that were causing the compression were cast out. I noticed that demons would leave my body and then return to talk to me on occasion and cause me pain. One time, a powerful demon returned to grieve me. He entered into me and then spoke to me at the same time he was giving me physical pain. He didn't stay long and then left my body. He didn't possess me but just oppressed me with pain.

Satan had just set up a scene within a dream. I was sound asleep during all of this. This reminded me of my dream world; after this, I knew Satan had controlled me for twenty-two years. The dream went something along these lines: It looks like sunset;

the orange and brownish surroundings of an unknown world stood out to me. Blade happened to appear within this dream. She was standing in a fighting pose, having a large sword in her left hand. Her long red hair flowed down her back. She was wearing tight black leather clothes, which covered her entire body, with a military look plastered across her face. As she was in this position, a young man was facing her in battle. As I was viewing this, King Tayten suddenly entered the scene. I wasn't controlling him within this dream. He walked slowly around the two and started to talk to the young man, pointing out to him how Blade was messing around, knowing full well she would win this battle. The young man was unaware that she was an excellent fighter out to destroy him. King Tayten introduced the idea to him.

He spoke to the young man and said, "She is slowly luring you over to her by allowing you to win."

My question was, who is King Tayten, actually? I always thought that I controlled the characters within my dream world. After this dream, it was evident that I wasn't alone inside my dream world. The characters came alive while you dreamed. You literally felt like you were having a conversation with them. Their gestures and movements within this state were so realistic. It felt like you were inside another world. It was extremely addictive; that's why I used to enter into it. It was like a rollercoaster ride: an adrenaline rush of excitement that gave me constant entertainment.

In this dream, King Tayten's personality was controlling, demanding, and firm towards Blade and this young man. He also wanted the young man to know Blade's plans.

King Tayten suddenly turned to this man and said, "If you run, I will throw a knife in your back."

The young man stood there looking at Blade in a confused, fearful state. Blade allowed the young man to cut her with the sword that was in his own hand; she acted like she was innocent and couldn't fight back. Suddenly, King Tayten started to walk away, and the dream ended.

One a separate day, I was lying in bed when a male voice entered my mind. He said, "Why do you hate me so much after I spent twenty-two years with you?" At the time, it sounded like Satan just spoke to me, but I refused to accept this because I had been confronting demons that were portraying to be the devil throughout the year. I didn't answer his question because the Lord blocked our conversation by sending me a Christian song.

My family and I decided to make a day out at the local markets. We arrived and started to walk around the place, looking at what people were selling. The last time I was here, I had a few demons compress my body with pain. I also noticed the fortune tellers around the place; I wanted to talk to one regarding Jesus. Fortune tellers deal with familiar spirits; they get their powers from the devil. It is an abomination if you seek after them. Although I wanted to do this, I got scared to approach them and backed off. I didn't want to make a scene. As I continued walking around the market, the Lord suddenly pulled me over towards a woman I just walked past. She was a fortune teller.

Stunned by what had happened, I quickly blurted out to her, "Come to Jesus because he's coming back soon."

The woman responded to my comment by saying that she was religious. As I spoke to her, my entire body started to become extremely nervous. It was the same type of nerves I felt as a child. I quickly realised that the demons were causing me to shake uncontrollably to keep me from talking to this woman about Jesus. It wasn't my anxiety or fear; I wasn't afraid to speak to her. I stopped talking and walked away from her, and my nerves disappeared.

As I went to sleep, I slipped into another dream state, but this time it was different. I was in a scene looking through my iPad when the images on the device turned to images of Satan. All of a sudden, I had this solid invisible form approach me within this dream. This being felt solid as a rock. I was on my bed when he approached me. I felt his form as he wrestled with me to have sex. I didn't win the fight, and he ended up sleeping with me within the dream. As he slept with me, he manifested into a man (I saw him on top of me but didn't witness anything else, neither did I feel anything sexual take place).

While in this state, this thought came to me: *Satan had just possessed a body and was sleeping with me.* However, on waking, I knew this wasn't Satan but a demon. I was upset and horrified at what just happened. I said, "Lord, please forgive me; this is not what I wanted." The Lord straight away sent two songs to conform me. The songs were "Soon and Very Soon We Are Going to See the King" and "Since Jesus Came into My Heart."

I had to take an exact dose of my medication, for my head pain was returning. However, it wasn't the same compressed pain that the demons had given me. This felt more natural. As I took the medication, I instantly received these words from a hymn. A spirit sung these words to me clearly. He sang, "All because *you* do not carry everything to God in prayer." I had to confess: I didn't pray at all that day, and I hadn't been praying much for months. God was telling me in a way that this was why I needed an extra dose of medication. Ever since the Lord started pulling me out of torment, I occasionally cried out to him. I speak to him every day and praise him for everything. After receiving those words, I straight away went to my knees and turned to the Lord and asked him to heal me and deliver me from the demons.

One busy morning, I was racing around, trying hard to get my child ready for school, when the Lord God reminded me to take her homework with me. I completely forgot about it. I was still struggling with my bad memory. When I forget, I completely forget things. My body was nearly completely healed now. I was happy again and feeling joyful. However, I was still not delivered from the demons. One night, I was lying on the bed, trying to fall asleep, when I felt this demon try to enter into me, but he was denied access to me. It felt like he bounced right off me.

"This is the first time I spoken to you," a male voice said to me as I was heading off to hang up the washing. "I'm the Lord your God."

I replied to him, "Did the Lord come in the flesh?"

He said, "I am the Lord."

I again asked him, "Did the Lord come in the flesh?"

He repeated to me that he was the Lord.

I again asked him, "Did the Lord come in the flesh?"

He went silent and eventually revealed that he was not the Lord.

I asked him, "Why did you not answer me straight away when I asked you if the Lord came in the flesh?"

The demon replied, "I didn't want to," and left.

One another day, I heard these words, "If you want, I'll get someone to pick you up," a demon said to me. This reminded me of a Christian testimony I once came across of a man who couldn't decide who to follow: Jesus or the devil. A demon spoke to this man and convinced him to serve Satan. He somehow ended up on this bus specifically full of people all wanting to serve the devil. They were all heading down the same road to worship Satan. While on board the bus, the Holy Spirit spoke to this man, strongly telling him to get off the bus. He hesitated at first but eventually got off. He ended up surrendering his life to Jesus.

I've read a lot of Christian testimonies. I want to share an incident with you regarding a Christian woman who claimed that she had communication with the devil. The story happened a few years ago. This woman received a text on her phone, demanding her to do something inappropriate. She thought it was strange because it was coming from the phone of one of her close friends. Her friend was also a Christian, and what she was asking was a random thing (she never did state what was demanded from her). She texted back and asked who it was. She was not convinced that it was her friend.

The text came back: "Satan," and he demanded her to do that particular thing that he asked of her.

She texted him back and said, "No! I believe in Jesus Christ."

The reply came back, "The Bible is a fairy tale, and I hate Jesus Christ."

She replied back and texted "No, the Bible is the Word of God, and Jesus Christ is Lord."

After sending this text, she never received a reply. She asked her friend about this; her friend said that she was at the movies with her phone off. It was in her purse the whole time. Her friend looked at her phone and found that no messages were sent to her friend at that time. Nothing in the inbox or outbox. This woman's conclusion was that Satan had spoken to her directly through text.

On a separate night, I was deep inside a dream when I found myself in this elaborate castle. I was on the upper level when I approached the balcony and looked down to the ground. I saw hundreds of people dressed in blue linen, with a cape flowing down their backs. I concluded that they were Satanists (I know now after waking that they weren't actually Satanists). A demon entered my dream and told me, "This is your last chance to witness to them about Jesus."

I started to shout out to the crowd of people that Jesus can save you. It really felt like I was actually talking to a real crowd. A lady came behind me (this was a demon), and I turned around and grabbed her arm.

I started to yell at her with intensity. I yelled, "You will never die for Satan. I would die for Jesus!" Straight after proclaiming these words, I came out of the dream.

Another time, I drifted off into a dream and found myself talking to a demon. I ended up saying something that wasn't pleasing to the Lord, so fear gripped me, and I had to apologise to the Lord while in this dreaming state. As I was dreaming, I asked the Lord if he could send me a song to know that I was still saved. Still within the dream, I asked a demon if the Lord came in the flesh. Instead of receiving an answer to my question, I heard a demon yell out to me, "I wanted you for a bride." Straight after these words were spoken, I felt myself slowly drift back into consciousness. As I returned and opened my eyes, I realised that this dream was so deep that the Lord blocked most of it. When I woke up, I instantly received a song from the Lord. He was confirming that I was indeed still saved.

My heart was being drawn towards the devil. I was constantly resisting the desire that they placed inside my heart. I was frustrated and annoyed again. I got on my knees to pray and asked the Lord to teach me to pray. As I started my prayer, the Lord took over and directed me.

I ended up saying, "I pray that I'm found worthy to escape from all the things that come on the Earth and stand before the son of man."

During prayer, the Lord also directed me to say that my heart wasn't quite right and to pray for this. I cried, for these words went straight through me. I knew that Satan had been trying to lure me over to him for almost two years now. I got up and headed out the door to pick up Violet from primary school. I got into the car and put on a CD and started to sing along. The Lord once again took over my voice, and I once again sang the song in Hebrew. I knew that I hit rock bottom, but the only way to go from there was up. I had faith in God and believed he was truly with me and would help me through this ordeal that had come upon me. As I got out of the car, I started to recall all the major sins that I'd done against God, and it added up. I couldn't believe how many evil things I had done against him. As I went through the list, I asked the Lord to forgive me for each one. I knew he already forgave me for all of my sins, but I still wanted to ask him for forgiveness. I believe that I've closed every doorway and repented, but I still have demons. My dreams weren't getting any better also. Only God can tell if the Lord will truly heal me from schizophrenia.

I want to explain that I don't like Satan. He tried to destroy my marriage, and tried to ruin my life. One time, I sinned greatly against God; still being in the world, I decided to stop this particular sin and proclaimed out loud, "I don't want Satan to take me down a darker road." I stopped that sin and repented from it and never looked back again. Shortly after I stopped this great sin, God decided he would also pull me out of the world itself, as well as the daydreaming world that I was involved in, so I could come to serve him completely. He helped me come back to him with all my heart, mind, soul, and strength. I'm now extremely glad he did, because I truly love the Lord.

There is a spiritual world, and if you believe in the Lord God, then you must believe in his word, which states that devils do exist. Being tormented the way I did left me in absolute pain, to the point where I sometimes wanted to die. When I did call to God in faith, he answered me, and he will answer you if you seek him with all your heart, mind, soul, and strength. I know that this is a controversial book; when I decided to write this book, I didn't know how it would turn out. I just wanted to share what I truly believe is the truth.

God knows that I have written this book, and while I wrote it, he showed me a vision of what he wanted me to take out of it. I tossed on what he showed me, for I knew it was the Lord who gave me this vision. I really didn't want to take the information out of my book, but I obeyed the Lord and removed it. My point is, God was with me while I was writing this book, and I truly hope you believe my testimony.

CHAPTER 16

THE ANTICHRIST

The Antichrist! A title that is well known in Christianity, but who exactly is this man, and where will he come from? The Bible is clear that there are many antichrists. These antichrists have come throughout our history and will continue to rise up. From the time of Nero onwards, Christians have suffered greatly under these antichrists. However, the final Antichrist, known as the son of perdition or the man of sin, is what I'll try to address to you in this chapter of my book.

"Little children, it is the last time: and as ye have heard that antichrist shall come, even now are there many antichrists; whereby we know that it is the last time." 1 John 2:18

Most people look at Rome, America, and even Israel when they refer to the Antichrist. However, when I started looking into this subject, it was the Middle East that caught my attention.

According to Daniel chapter 8, the Antichrist comes out of one of Alexander the Great's four generals' kingdoms. After the death of Alexander the Great, his four generals, known as the *Diadochoi* (successors), finally divided the empire into four divisions. These four generals were:

- Ptolemy: ruled over Egypt, Peterea, Palestine, and Arabia
- Seleucus (Seleucid Empire): ruled over Babylon, assisting Ptolemy until he was forced out by Antigonus, who ruled over Babylon, Syria, and central Asia
- Lysimachus: ruled over Bythinia and Thrace
- Cassander: ruled over Greece and Macedonia

Let's look at scripture to support this claim.

"Therefore the he goat waxed very great: and when he was strong, the great horn was broken; and for it came up four notable ones toward the four winds of heaven. And out of one of them came forth a little horn, which waxed exceeding great, toward the south, and toward the east, and toward the pleasant land." (Daniel 8:8–9)

Who is the goat, the great horn, the four notable ones?

"And the rough goat is the king of Grecia: and the great horn that is between his eyes is the first king [Alexander the Great]. Now that being broken [Alexander the Great dies], whereas four stood up for it [these are the four generals of Alexander the Great mentioned above] four kingdoms shall stand up out of the nation, but not in his power." (Daniel 8:21)

Out of one of these four kingdoms of Alexander the Great, four generals will come, the Antichrist, also known as the little horn.

"And out of one of them came forth a little horn, which waxed exceeding great, toward the south, and toward the east, and toward the pleasant land." (Daniel 8:9)

"And in the latter time of their kingdom [the four generals of Alexander the Great], when the transgressors are come to the full, a king of fierce countenance, and understanding dark sentences, shall stand up." (Daniel 8:23)

This king called the little horn is the Antichrist. How do we find out which of these four generals' kingdoms will be the one that the Antichrist comes out of?

The Bible calls the Antichrist "Gog" and says he comes out of the land of Magog:

"Son of man, set thy face against Gog, the land of Magog, the chief prince of Meshech and Tubal, and prophesy against him, And say, Thus saith the Lord GOD; Behold, I am against thee, O Gog, the chief prince of Meshech and Tuba." (Ezekiel 38:2–3)

Most Christians believe that Magog is Russia, but after some research, I found that Meshech, Tubal, and the land of Magog were once located in the northern parts of the Middle East. Iraq, Syria, and Turkey are all located in the north of the Middle East. It seems fit to say that the Antichrist will rise out of the north of the Middle East, which would be the Seleucid Empire.

"Therefore, thou son of man, prophesy against Gog, and say, Thus saith the Lord GOD; Behold, I am against thee, O Gog, the chief prince of Meshech and Tubal: And I will turn thee back, and leave but the sixth part of thee, and will cause thee to come up from the north parts, and will bring thee upon the mountains of Israel." (Ezekiel 38:1–2)

According to the Bible, the Antichrist or Gog will invade Israel with the help of the following countries:

- Persia (Iran)
- Ethiopia
- Libya

The Bible also mentions names like

- Gomer and all his bands
- the house of Togarmah of the north quarters and all his bands

If we look up Gomer and Togarmah in the Bible, we come to the sons of Japheth from 1 Chronicles. The names Magog, Tubal, and Meshech also are revealed to us.

"The sons of Japheth; Gomer, and Magog, and Madai, and Javan, and Tubal, and Meshech, and Tiras. And the sons of Gomer;

Ashchenaz, and Riphath, and Togarmah. And the sons of Javan; Elishah, and Tarshish, Kittim, and Dodanim." (1 Chronicles 1:5–7)

Keeping with scripture, the land of Magog has to be located in one of Alexander the Great's four generals' kingdoms. Rome is not part of these four kingdoms; neither is Russia.

I really can't say where Gomer and the house of Togarmah are located in today's countries. This is my own theory, but I believe that they are in the Middle East. Some maps show that Gomer, Magog, Meshech, Tubal, and Togarmah are located in Turkey.

Will the Antichrist invade Israel? Yes, he will. Let's look at a few scripture verses to support this:

"And out of one of them came forth a little horn, which waxed exceeding great, toward the south, and toward the east, and toward the pleasant land." (Daniel 8:9)

The pleasant land is Israel's land. As you can see from the above verse, the Antichrist expands his kingdom towards the south of the Middle East, east of the Middle East, and then towards Israel itself.

The Antichrist will take an army to Israel, surround Jerusalem, and take it captive.

"And when ye shall see Jerusalem compassed with armies, then know that the desolation thereof is nigh." (Luke 21:20)

Our Lord Jesus warns us in Matthew 24, Luke 21, and Mark 13 about the end times. Please read these chapters to receive a better understanding of what I'm trying to show you.

When the Antichrist enters into Israel with his army, he does the following things:

- They pollute the temple.
- He stops the daily sacrifices and oblations in the temple.
- They set up the abomination that maketh desolate.

"And arms shall stand on his part, and they shall pollute the sanctuary of strength, and shall take away the daily sacrifice, and they shall place the abomination that maketh desolate." (Daniel 11:31)

What is the abomination that maketh desolate? I've thought about this a lot, and the only thing I can see is that the Antichrist might be the abomination that maketh desolate.

Look at these verses to determine this:

"And he [the Antichrist] shall confirm the covenant with many for one week: and in the midst of the week he shall cause the sacrifice and the oblation to cease, and for the overspreading of abominations he [Antichrist] shall make it desolate, even until the consummation, and that determined shall be poured upon the desolate." (Daniel 9:27)

"When ye therefore shall see the abomination of desolation, spoken of by Daniel the prophet, stand in the holy place (whoso readeth, let him understand)." (Matthew 24:15)

The Antichrist will claim to be God and exalt himself above every God; this would include Allah. He will sit in the third temple, showing himself that he is God.

"Let no man deceive you by any means: for that day shall not come, except there come a falling away first, and that man of sin be revealed, the son of perdition; Who opposeth and exalteth himself above all that is called God, or that is worshipped; so that he as God sitteth in the temple of God, shewing himself that he is God." (2 Thessalonians 2:3–4)

Now this is when things get a bit more complicated: We are given three time periods in the book of Daniel:

We are given 1,290 days, 1,335 days, and 2,300 days.

The 1,290 days equals approximately 3.5 years.

The 1,335 days equals 3.6 years.

The 2,300 days equals 6.3 years.

What are these timelines for? Let's take a look:

"And from the time that the daily sacrifice shall be taken away, and the abomination that maketh desolate set up, there shall be a thousand two hundred and ninety days [1,290 days or 3.5 years]." (Daniel 12:11)

What happens in this 3.5-year time frame after the abomination that maketh desolation is set up? According to the Bible, it is when the Great Tribulation will occur.

"When ye therefore shall see the abomination of desolation, spoken of by Daniel the prophet, stand in the holy place (whoso readeth, let him understand:)

Then let them which be in Judaea flee into the mountains:

Let him which is on the housetop not come down to take any thing out of his house:

Neither let him which is in the field return back to take his clothes.

And woe unto them that are with child, and to them that give suck in those days!

But pray ye that your flight be not in the winter, neither on the sabbath day:

For then shall be great tribulation, such as was not since the beginning of the world to this time, no, nor ever shall be." (Matthew 24:15–21)

"And he [the Antichrist] shall speak great words against the most High, and shall wear out the saints [Christians/messianic Jews] of the most High [our Father in heaven], and think to change times and laws: and they [saints] shall be given into his [the Antichrist's] hand until a time and times and the dividing of time [3.5 years]." (Daniel 7:25)

The Antichrist will be given power over all nations and nationalities of the world.

"And it was given unto him [the Antichrist] to make war with the saints, and to overcome them: and power was given him over all kindreds, and tongues, and nations." (Revelation 13:7)

Most people believe in a pre-tribulation rapture, but according to God's word, the rapture happens when the Lord returns; this is the day of the Lord. Jesus will come after the Great Tribulation occurs. Look at these verses:

"Let no man deceive you by any means: for that day shall not come, except there come a falling away first, and that man of sin be revealed, the son of perdition." (2 Thessalonians 2:3)

"Immediately after the tribulation of those days shall the sun be darkened, and the moon shall not give her light, and the stars shall fall from heaven, and the powers of the heavens shall be shaken: And then shall appear the sign of the Son of man in heaven: and then shall all the tribes of the earth mourn, and they shall see the Son of man coming in the clouds of heaven with power and great glory. And he shall send his angels with a great sound of a trumpet, and they shall gather together his elect_from the four winds, from one end of heaven to the other." (Matthew 24:29–31)

"But in those days, after that tribulation, the sun shall be darkened, and the moon shall not give her light, And the stars of heaven shall fall, and the powers that are in heaven shall be shaken. And then shall they see the Son of man coming in the clouds with great power and glory. And then shall he send his angels, and shall gather together his elect from the four winds, from the uttermost part of the earth to the uttermost part of heaven." (Mark 13:24–27)

I'm not sure what this 1,335 days might be, but the Lord states that whosoever waits and comes to this time period is blessed.

"Blessed is he that waiteth, and cometh to the thousand three hundred and five and thirty days [1,335 days, or 3.6 years]." (Daniel 12:12)

Now let's look at the last time period in the book of Daniel: the 2,300 days or 6.3 years.

"Yea, he magnified himself even to the prince of the host, and by him the daily sacrifice was taken away, and the place of the sanctuary was cast down.

And an host was given him against the daily sacrifice by reason of transgression, and it cast down the truth to the ground; and it practised, and prospered." (Daniel 8:11–12)

"Then I heard one saint speaking, and another saint said unto that certain saint which spake, How long shall be the vision concerning the daily sacrifice, and the transgression of desolation, to give both the sanctuary and the host to be trodden under foot?

And he said unto me, Unto two thousand and three hundred days; then shall the sanctuary be cleansed." (Daniel 8:13–14)

I believe that there are 6.3 years from when the daily sacrifices cease and the transgression of desolation is set up. After 6.3 years, the temple is cleansed, and the host is destroyed.

What is the host? I could be wrong, but I believe it is a spiritual being of some sort. It could be the Beast of Revelation 17:8; I really don't believe the host is Satan.

"The beast that thou sawest was, and is not; and shall ascend out of the bottomless pit, and go into perdition: and they that dwell on the earth shall wonder, whose names were not written in the book of life from the foundation of the world, when they behold the beast that was, and is not, and yet is." (Revelation 17:8)

Most Christians believe that Satan will enter into the Antichrist just like he did with Judas Iscariot.

"Then entered Satan into Judas surnamed Iscariot, being of the number of the twelve." (Luke 22:3)

However, when I read Revelation, I see that Satan is the one that gives the Beast all its power and appears separate from the Beast.

"And the beast which I saw was like unto a leopard, and his feet were as the feet of a bear, and his mouth as the mouth of a lion: and the dragon [Satan] gave him his power, and his seat, and great authority." (Revelation 13:2)

"And they worshipped the dragon [Satan] which gave power unto the beast: and they worshipped the beast, saying, Who is like unto the beast? who is able to make war with him?"

(Revelation 13:4)

"And I saw three unclean spirits like frogs come out of the mouth of the dragon [Satan], and out of the mouth of the beast, and out of the mouth of the false prophet." (Revelation 16:13)

Let me explain the Beast to you. I believe there are three parts to the Beast.

The Beast will be the:

- fourth kingdom
- king
- spiritual being

In the books of Daniel and Revelation, the Beast is revealed to us:

"After this I saw in the night visions, and behold a fourth beast, dreadful and terrible, and strong exceedingly; and it had great iron teeth: it devoured and brake in pieces, and stamped the residue with the feet of it: and it was diverse from all the beasts that were before it; and it had ten horns.

I considered the horns, and, behold, there came up among them another little horn, before whom there were three of the first horns plucked up by the roots: and, behold, in this horn were eyes like the eyes of man, and a mouth speaking great things." (Daniel 7:7–8)

"And I stood upon the sand of the sea, and saw a beast rise up out of the sea, having seven heads and ten horns, and upon his horns ten crowns, and upon his heads the name of blasphemy. And the beast which I saw was like unto a leopard, and his feet were as the feet of a bear, and his mouth as the mouth of a lion: and the dragon [Satan] gave him his power, and his seat, and great authority." (Revelation 13:1–2)

This is the description of the Beast. The Beast is complicated; when you look at the animals that make up the Beast, we have the following:

- a lion
- a bear
- a leopard

We find these animals in the book of Daniel chapter 7. These are three of the four kingdoms that have risen in the earth throughout history:

- Lion is Babylon.
- Bear is Medo-Persia.
- Leopard is Grecia.

This fourth Beast is the fourth kingdom on the earth, known as "the dreadful and terrible beast." This Beast (kingdom) is powerful and has ten kings, which represent the ten horns. The Antichrist or little horn comes among these ten kings and uproots three of them. This fourth kingdom will devour the whole earth.

"Thus he said, The fourth beast shall be the fourth kingdom upon earth, which shall be diverse from all kingdoms, and shall devour the whole earth, and shall tread it down, and break it in pieces. And the ten horns out of this kingdom are ten kings that shall arise: and another shall rise after them [this would be the Antichrist]; and he shall be diverse from the first, and he shall subdue three kings." (Daniel 7:23–2)

"I considered the horns, and, behold, there came up among them another little horn, before whom there were three of the first horns plucked up by the roots: and, behold, in this horn were eyes like the eyes of man, and a mouth speaking great things." (Daniel 7:8)

Like I mentioned earlier, the Beast is also a king, according to the Bible.

"These great beasts, which are four, are four kings, which shall arise out of the earth." (Daniel 7:17)

I believe that the four kings are:

- King Nebuchadnezzar (first kingdom: Babylon)
- Cyrus the Great (second kingdom: Medo-Persia)
- Alexander the Great (third kingdom: Grecia)
- The Antichrist (fourth kingdom: ?)

I tried to look at the seven heads that are attached to the Beast in Revelation 13, but you need wisdom to solve this puzzle. The Lord Jesus one day rebuked me during prayer for posting up a You

Tube video on the seven heads. I got it completely wrong. I had to take down the video and start again. I still can't solve this problem.

The false prophet; who is this? According to the Bible, the false prophet is the one who wrought miracles before the Beast and deceived the people, who took the mark of the Beast and worshipped the image of the Beast.

"And the beast was taken, and with him the false prophet that wrought miracles before him, with which he deceived them that had received the mark of the beast, and them that worshipped his image. These both were cast alive into a lake of fire burning with brimstone." (Revelation 19:20)

If we look at Revelation 13:11–18, we can see another Beast rising out of the earth having two horns like a lamb and speaking like a dragon. This is the false prophet's description. The false prophet exercises all the power of the Beast. We can see that the Beast will have power over all nations of the world. The false prophet makes the entire world worship the Beast; if we remember, the Antichrist claims to be God. The false prophet does miracles and wonders to deceive the people. The false prophet also causes the world to make an image to the Beast. I'm not sure what the image of the Beast will be. It could be a hidden meaning that represents this. However, people who don't worship the image of the beast will be killed. The false prophet also causes all people, young or old, to take the mark of the beast on their right hand or forehead; you can't buy or sell unless you have this mark.

This mark: The name of the beast or the number of the name of it is six hundred (600) and sixty (60)-six (6); everyone know it as 666. The Hebrew alphabet for 600 is *Sofit* (Final) *Mem*, 60 is *Semekh*, and 6 is *Vav*. In Greek, it is *Chi Xi Digamma*. I not sure how you would count the number of the beast; the Bible states that it's a man's number. This would be the Antichrist's name and number that is placed within this mark. As we head into the future, our society is becoming cashless. Bank cards that allow us to simply tap and go are becoming more and more common. I work in an office that deals with money, and I can tell you that more people are using their cards rather than cash. Only the future will tell us what the mark of the Beast will actually be. If it is an insert that is placed under our skins, like an RFID chip, only time can tell. However, be alert and don't take this mark. Let's say this mark does come out, and you live to see it. It will cripple you because you can't go shopping unless you have this mark; you wouldn't be able to eat or travel. Even using your car, you need petrol. It will be devastating to be a Christian at these horrific times. However, we need to stay strong and never deny our Lord, even until the death. The end result is far worse than death itself.

"And he causeth all, both small and great, rich and poor, free and bond, to receive a mark in their right hand, or in their foreheads: And that no man might buy or sell, save he that had the mark, or the name of the beast, or the number of his name. Here is wisdom. Let him that hath understanding count the number of the beast: for it is the number of a man; and his number is Six hundred threescore and six." (Revelation 13:16–18)

The Bible also states that anyone who worships the beast and the image of the beast and receives a mark on the forehead or upon the hand of him will get the wrath of God poured without mixture.

"The same shall drink of the wine of the wrath of God, which is poured out without mixture into the cup of his indignation; and he shall be tormented with fire and brimstone in the presence of the holy angels, and in the presence of the Lamb: And the smoke of their torment ascendeth up forever and ever: and they have no rest day nor night, who worship the beast and his image, and whosoever receiveth the mark of his name." (Revelation 14:10–11)

It's not just the mark of the beast that you need to be concerned with. It's also worshipping the image of the beast and the beast itself and receiving the mark of his name. The Bible is complicated, but this is a warning to all: read the Bible and piece together scripture with what matches.

"For precept must be upon precept, precept upon precept; line upon line, line upon line; here a little, and there a little." (Isaiah 28:10)

What will happen to the Beast, false prophet, and Satan? According to the Bible, Jesus will return to the Earth with his army (his saints). He destroys the armies of the nations that are gathered together to battle him (this is at Armageddon). The false prophet and the Beast are captured and thrown in the lake of fire, and Satan is bound with a chain by an angel and thrown in the bottomless pit (hell) for a thousand years. I believe that this is when the day of the Lord takes place.

"And I saw heaven opened, and behold a white horse; and he [Jesus] that sat upon him was called Faithful and True, and in righteousness he doth judge and make war. His eyes were as a flame of fire, and on his head were many crowns; and he had a name written, that no man knew, but he himself. And he was clothed with a vesture dipped in blood: and his name is called The Word of God. And the armies which were in heaven followed him upon white horses [the saints of God], clothed in fine linen, white and clean. And out of his [Jesus] mouth goeth a sharp sword, that with it he should smite the nations: and he shall rule them with a rod of iron: and he treadeth the winepress of the fierceness and wrath of Almighty God. And he hath on his vesture and on his thigh a name written, KING OF KINGS, AND LORD OF LORDS. And I saw an angel standing in the sun; and he cried with a loud voice, saying to all the fowls that fly in the midst of heaven, Come and gather yourselves together unto the supper of the great God; That ye may eat the flesh of kings, and the flesh of captains, and the flesh of mighty men, and the flesh of horses, and of them that sit on them, and the flesh of all men, both free and bond, both small and great. And I saw the beast, and the kings of the earth, and their armies, gathered together to make war against him that sat on the horse, and against his army. And the beast was taken, and with him the false prophet that wrought miracles before him, with which he deceived them that had received the mark of the beast, and them that worshipped his image. These both were cast alive into a lake of fire burning with brimstone. And the remnant were slain with the sword of him that sat upon the horse, which sword proceeded out of his mouth: and all the fowls were filled with their flesh." (Revelation 19:11–21)

"And I saw an angel come down from heaven, having the key of the bottomless pit and a great chain in his hand. And he laid hold on the dragon, that old serpent, which is the Devil, and Satan, and bound him a thousand years, And cast him into the bottomless pit, and shut him up, and set a seal upon him, that he should deceive the nations no more, till the thousand years should be fulfilled: and after that he must be loosed a little season." (Revelation 20:1–3)

Jesus then rules the Earth for a thousand years with his saints.

"And I saw thrones, and they sat upon them, and judgment was given unto them: and I saw the souls of them that were beheaded for the witness of Jesus, and for the word of God, and which had not worshipped the beast, neither his image, neither had received his mark upon their foreheads, or in their hands; and they lived and reigned with Christ a thousand years." (Revelation 20:4)

I haven't mentioned everything that will happen, but only given you a glimpse of the future events surrounding Israel and the world when the Antichrist does come to the scene.

CHAPTER 17

REVELATION 12

I WANT TO LOOK at Revelation chapter 12 regarding events that have already taken place and those that will take place, according to the Bible. I will also go through each verse from Revelation 12 and try my best to explain them.

"And there appeared a great wonder in heaven; a woman clothed with the sun, and the moon under her feet, and upon her head a crown of twelve stars." (Revelation 12:1)

Who is this woman? According to the Bible, this woman is the nation of Israel. The twelve stars represent the twelve tribes of Israel, and the moon and sun relate to Joseph's dream. This is a picture of Jacob (Israel), Rebecca, and the twelve tribes of Israel.

"And he dreamed yet another dream, and told it his brethren, and said, Behold, I have dreamed a dream more; and, behold, the sun and the moon and the eleven stars made obeisance to me. And he told it to his father, and to his brethren: and his father rebuked him, and said unto him, What is this dream that thou hast dreamed? Shall I and thy mother and thy brethren indeed come to bow down ourselves to thee to the earth?" (Genesis 37:9–10)

"And she being with child cried, travailing in birth, and pained to be delivered." (Revelation 12:2)

This verse tells us that Israel was ready to bring forth her child. The child is the Messiah: Jesus.

"And there appeared another wonder in heaven; and behold a great red dragon, having seven heads and ten horns, and seven crowns upon his heads." (Revelation 12:3)

In this verse, the dragon (who is Satan) appears in heaven. Satan gives the Beast its power, authority, and seat. He holds the seven heads, ten horns, and seven crowns.

"And his tail drew the third part of the stars of heaven, and did cast them to the earth: and the dragon stood before the woman which was ready to be delivered, for to devour her child as soon as it was born." (Revelation 12:4)

Satan, not Lucifer, drew a third of the angels of heaven, and he cast them to the earth. Satan wanted to devour the Messiah (who is Jesus), as soon as he was born. If we look at Matthew chapter 2, we see King Herod wanting to kill Jesus by tricking the wise men into sending him word of his whereabouts.

"Then Herod, when he had privily called the wise men, enquired of them diligently what time the star appeared. And he sent them to Bethlehem, and said, Go and search diligently for the young child; and when ye have found him, bring me word again, that I may come and worship him also." (Matthew 2:7–8)

"And when they were departed, behold, the angel of the Lord appeareth to Joseph in a dream, saying, Arise, and take the young child and his mother, and flee into Egypt, and be thou there until I bring thee word: for Herod will seek the young child to destroy him. When he arose, he took the young child and his mother by night, and departed into Egypt." (Matthew 2:13–14)

"And she brought forth a man child, who was to rule all nations with a rod of iron: and her child was caught up unto God, and to his throne." (Revelation 12:5)

The nation of Israel brought forth the Messiah, who was and is Jesus Christ. He was to rule all nations with a rod of iron. However, he was betrayed and crucified on the cross. After three days, God raised him from the dead. Being seen by the apostles and the saints of God, he then ascended up to heaven and is now seated on the right hand of God. Jesus was given all power and authority. However, the Lord Jesus will return to rule with a rod of iron at his second coming.

"And the woman fled into the wilderness, where she hath a place prepared of God, that they should feed her there a thousand two hundred and threescore days." (Revelation 12:6)

The woman, who is Israel, flees into the wilderness for 1,260 days, where God takes care of her. The only other place that the 1,260 days is mentioned in the Bible is when the two witnesses or the two anointed ones start to prophecy for 1,260 days. I believe they are two prophets who stand before the God of all the earth.

"And I will give power unto my two witnesses, and they shall prophesy a thousand two hundred and threescore days, clothed in sackcloth." (Revelation 11:3)

I wonder if the dates are done this way to recognised that Israel will flee into the wilderness for approximately 3.4 years. During their prophecy, the two witnesses will cause there to be plagues on the earth and no rain, as well as to turn the water into blood.

"These have power to shut heaven, that it rain not in the days of their prophecy: and have power over waters to turn them to blood, and to smite the earth with all plagues, as often as they will." (Revelation 11:6)

The Beast will make war against the two witnesses. The Beast will kill them at the end of the 1,260-day time period (3.4 years). This will happen before the Great Tribulation occurs.

"And when they shall have finished their testimony, the beast that ascendeth out of the bottomless pit shall make war against them, and shall overcome them, and kill them." (Revelation 11:7)

"And there was war in heaven: Michael and his angels fought against the dragon; and the dragon fought and his angels, And prevailed not; neither was their place found any more in heaven. And the great dragon was cast out, that old serpent, called the Devil, and

Satan, which deceiveth the whole world: he was cast out into the earth, and his angels were cast out with him." (Revelation 12:7–9)

The war mentioned above hasn't happened yet. Satan is the dragon, and Michael is one of God's angels. Satan and his angels fight against Michael and his angels. However, Satan doesn't win the war and is cast to the earth, along with his angels. They no longer have a place in heaven.

"And I heard a loud voice saying in heaven, Now is come salvation, and strength, and the kingdom of our God, and the power of his Christ: for the accuser of our brethren is cast down, which accused them before our God day and night." (Revelation 12:10)

Satan is the accuser. This is clearly demonstrated in the book of Job.

"And the Lord said unto Satan, Hast thou considered my servant Job, that there is none like him in the earth, a perfect and an upright man, one that feareth God, and escheweth evil? Then Satan answered the Lord, and said, Doth Job fear God for nought? Hast not thou made an hedge about him, and about his house, and about all that he hath on every side? thou hast blessed the work of his hands, and his substance is increased in the land. But put forth thine hand now, and touch all that he hath, and he will curse thee to thy face." (Job 1:8–11)

In this chapter of Job, we can clearly see that Satan wasn't cast out of heaven yet. Satan has access to enter heaven. He also is able to stand before God and his angels. I believe that the dragon, who is Satan, is cast out of heaven just before the Great Tribulation occurs. I'll try and prove this to you by looking at the rest of Revelation chapter 12 and the book of Daniel.

"Now there was a day when the sons of God came to present themselves before the Lord, and Satan came also among them. And the Lord said unto Satan, Whence comest thou? Then Satan answered the Lord, and said, From going to and fro in the earth, and from walking up and down in it." (Job 1:6–7)

"And they overcame him by the blood of the Lamb, and by

the word of their testimony; and they loved not their lives unto the death. Therefore rejoice, ye heavens, and ye that dwell in them. Woe to the inhabiters of the earth and of the sea! for the devil is come down unto you, having great wrath, because he knoweth that he hath but a short time." (Revelation 12:11–12)

They overcame Satan by the blood of Jesus and the word of their testimony, and they loved not their lives to the death. I believe these are the true born-again Christians and messianic Jews. They are willing to die for Jesus, no matter what happens to them. Satan is now no longer able to access heaven and is cast to the Earth. He has a short time left and has great wrath. What does he do?

"And when the dragon saw that he was cast unto the earth, he persecuted the woman which brought forth the man child. And to the woman were given two wings of a great eagle, that she might fly into the wilderness, into her place, where she is nourished for a time, and times, and half a time, from the face of the serpent. And the serpent cast out of his mouth water as a flood after the woman, that he might cause her to be carried away of the flood. And the earth helped the woman, and the earth opened her mouth, and swallowed up the flood which the dragon cast out of his mouth." (Revelation 12:13–16)

We have Satan now cast to the earth; he brings on the Great Tribulation. Satan firstly tries to persecute the nation of Israel. Those who flee into the wilderness are taken care of for 3.5 years. If we look in the Bible for the phrase "time, and times, and half a time," it leads us to the Great Tribulation time period of 3.5 years or time, times, and half a time. Let's take a look at the verses below:

"And at that time shall Michael stand up, the great prince which standeth for the children of thy people: and there shall be a time of trouble, such as never was since there was a nation even to that same time: and at that time thy people shall be delivered, every one that shall be found written in the book." (Daniel 12:1)

"And I heard the man clothed in linen, which was upon the waters of the river, when he held up his right hand and his left hand unto heaven, and sware by him that liveth for ever that it shall be for a time, times, and an half; and when he shall have accomplished to scatter the power of the holy people, all these things shall be finished. And I heard, but I understood not: then said I, O my Lord, what shall be the end of these things? And he said, Go thy way, Daniel: for the words are closed up and sealed till the time of the end. Many shall be purified, and made white, and tried; but the wicked shall do wickedly: and none of the wicked shall understand; but the wise shall understand. And from the time that the daily sacrifice shall be taken away, and the abomination that maketh desolate set up, there shall be a thousand two hundred and ninety days [3.5 years]." (Daniel 12:7–11)

"And he [the Antichrist] shall speak great words against the most High, and shall wear out the saints of the most High, and think to change times and laws: and they shall be given into his hand until a time and times and the dividing of time." (Daniel 7:25)

"And the dragon was wroth with the woman, and went to make war with the remnant of her seed, which keep the commandments of God, and have the testimony of Jesus Christ." (Revelations 12:17)

If we examine the above verse, we see that Satan's anger with Israel is now turned towards the "Christians." Satan makes war with the remnant of her seed. I believe "the remnant of her seed" are the true born-again Christians: those who kept the testimony of Jesus and the commandments of God.

CHAPTER 18

SIN

All unrighteousness is sin. However, sin not only affects human beings, it also affects angels as well as the kingdom of darkness (this would include Satan).

Lucifer, who was perfected from the day he was created, was affected by sin. Iniquity was found in him, and he became violent, causing him to sin.

"By the multitude of thy merchandise they have filled the midst of thee with violence, and thou hast sinned." (Ezekiel 28:16)

"Thou wast perfect in thy ways from the day that thou wast created, till iniquity was found in thee." (Ezekiel 28:15)

As a result, he was cast to the ground by the Lord and is probably in hell, like the other angels that are kept under darkness until the judgement of the great day. Darkness is Satan's domain.

"And the angels which kept not their first estate, but left their own habitation, he hath reserved in everlasting chains under darkness unto the judgment of the great day." (Jude 1:6)

For if God spared not the angels that sinned, but cast them down to hell, and delivered them into chains of darkness, to be reserved unto judgment; (2 Peter 2:4)

These angels that are kept under darkness are the angels that left heaven and came to the Earth to take themselves wives from the children of men. They sinned and now are locked in hell with everlasting chains.

"And it came to pass, when men began to multiply on the face of the earth, and daughters were born unto them, That the sons of God saw the daughters of men that they were fair; and they took them wives of all which they chose." (Genesis 6:1–2)

The devil sinned from the beginning. Anyone who commits sin is of the devil.

"He that committeth sin is of the devil; for the devil sinneth from the beginning. For this purpose the Son of God was manifested, that he might destroy the works of the devil." (1 John 3:8)

Sin entered into the Earth by one man, this man was Adam. He disobeyed God by eating the fruit from the tree of the knowledge of good and evil; as a result, death passed upon everyone.

"Wherefore, as by one man sin entered into the world, and death by sin; and so death passed upon all men, for that all have sinned." (Romans 5:12)

If we willingly do wrong, it is sin. For the strength of sin is the law, and by the law we know what sin is.

"All unrighteousness is sin: and there is a sin not unto death." (1 John 5:17)

"What shall we say then? Is the law sin? God forbid. Nay, I had not known sin, but by the law: for I had not known lust, except the law had said, Thou shalt not covet." (Romans 7:7)

Sin lies at the door and has a desire to rule over you. However, we have to rule over sin and not let it rule over us.

"If thou doest well, shalt thou not be accepted? and if thou doest not well, sin lieth at the door. And unto thee shall be his desire, and thou shalt rule over him." (Genesis 4:7)

The Bible teaches that all have sinned and fall short of the glory of God.

"For all have sinned, and come short of the glory of God." (Romans 3:23)

The word of God (Jesus) came to the Earth in the form of sinful flesh. Jesus committed no sin and was a spotless lamb to God: perfect and without blemish. He was the ultimate sacrifice and was offered once to bear the sins of many.

"For what the law could not do, in that it was weak through the flesh, God sending his own Son in the likeness of sinful flesh, and for sin, condemned sin in the flesh." (Romans 8:3)

"So Christ was once offered to bear the sins of many; and unto them that look for him shall he appear the second time without sin unto salvation." (Hebrews 9:28)

"But with the precious blood of Christ, as of a lamb without blemish and without spot." (Peter 1:19)

By Adam, many were made sinners. However, because Jesus was obedient, by him, many are now made righteous and are given eternal life through our Lord Jesus.

"For as by one man's disobedience many were made sinners, so by the obedience of one shall many be made righteous." (Romans 5:19)

"That as sin hath reigned unto death, even so might grace reign through righteousness unto eternal life by Jesus Christ our Lord." (Romans 5:21)

This is why it is important to repent from all our sins and to live a righteous life. We can only renew our minds by the help of the Holy Spirit, who lives in us. We choose to either obey God or disobey him.

God wants to save the world. If you believe in Jesus, then there is no condemnation. However, if you do not believe in him, you're already condemned. The end result is that you will spend the rest of your eternity in the lake of fire. The Bible teaches that people like darkness rather than light because of their evil deeds, so expose your sins and repent. God is faithful and just to forgive us of our sins.

"For God so loved the world, that he gave his only begotten

Son, that whosoever believeth in him should not perish, but have everlasting life. For God sent not his Son into the world to condemn the world; but that the world through him might be saved. He that believeth on him is not condemned: but he that believeth not is condemned already, because he hath not believed in the name of the only begotten Son of God. And this is the condemnation, that light is come into the world, and men loved darkness rather than light, because their deeds were evil. For every one that doeth evil hateth the light, neither cometh to the light, lest his deeds should be reproved. But he that doeth truth cometh to the light, that his deeds may be made manifest, that they are wrought in God." (John 3:16–21)

"If we confess our sins, he is faithful and just to forgive us our sins, and to cleanse us from all unrighteousness." (1 John 1:9)

CONCLUSION

Our Lord is gracious and merciful. The key to a good relationship with God through Jesus Christ our Lord is to truly repent and turn away from all evil and worldly involvement. Confess your sins and asked the Lord for forgiveness. Most of all, don't be a hearer of his word only, but a doer. God wants to save the lost. Seek God and read the Bible on a daily basis and meditate on what you read and ask God to give you understanding. The key to understanding scripture is to read what is actually written and piece together what matches. Jesus is the truth, and there is no other way to God but through him.

"Jesus saith unto him, I am the way, the truth, and the life: no man cometh unto the Father, but by me." (John 14:6)

He is the road to salvation. There is no other way.

I wrote the following poem during my time of extreme torment; it describes how the Lord set me free:

<u>Set Free</u>

I was deep in darkness.
No light I saw.
Many years I spent behind closed doors.
I turned myself away from him,
Christ Jesus,
my risen King.

Deep in sin,
I was stained.
No one else but me to blame.
The devil tried to take my life.
He set me on a course.
He had absolutely no remorse.
It wasn't until God stepped in,
removing all these hidden sins,
that I'm now sanctified, justified, and called.
Eternal life is now my great reward.

Printed in the United States
By Bookmasters